Book Cover and illustrations by Kristen S. Keller
Edition One 2024

Contents

Foreword

In the thick of a sunny yet frigid Colorado morning, I sat in the kitchen of my mountain home, where dim winter light filtered through frost-rimmed windows; the glowing fireplace holding my mood stable.

Scattered across the heavy oak table lay a sea of legal papers, their stark white presence a contrast to the warmth of my surroundings. The harsh words spoken by my lawyer shattered the mountain stillness: "Despite maintaining your innocence, you could risk thirty years of your life if you lose at trial, or you can accept this plea deal of 6-8 years in the Department of Corrections..."

My life, once defined by relentless ambition as a Licensed Professional Counselor, had skid off course into a chaos I could hardly recognize as my own. I had been derailed by allegations I fiercely disputed but could not escape. The justice system's ultimatum forced an unimaginable decision: gamble with decades of my life to fight or accept a punishment for something I didn't do.

During these darkest hours, trapped in a broken system that threatened to end my career and freedom; I realized I had a choice. I could be crushed by the weight of this injustice or rise above it, leveraging my knowledge and resilience to create a path to healing for myself and my loved ones.

"Everything happens for a reason," I whispered to myself, recalling my mother's lifelong wisdom. "Everything, happens for a reason."

This time, it was my turn in the chair.

But, the road ahead was long. It was filled with challenges, setbacks, and moments when giving up seemed easier than pushing forward. I wanted to quit. But somehow, I didn't. Through it all, I held onto hope and maintained a positive attitude. I embraced every struggle and every obstacle, knowing it was part of my journey.

Power of Healing Trauma was born not from theory, but from survival. It's the map I made while crawling out from the hole I dug, and also fell into. Now I'm handing the map to you.

Trauma has been my companion since I was young. At 15, I nearly died in a car crash. Our vehicle slammed into a ditch at 120 miles per hour when the gas pedal stuck. The crash brought me inches from death's door. Literally. I experienced seeing the 'light' that so many speak of, but few encounter. As I hovered above my body, I watched the emergency room personnel swiftly cutaway my clothing, my consciousness floating peacefully in the distance. Then, in an instant, I was sucked back into my physical form with the force of a powerful vacuum, crashing onto the table below. For months, I thought it had all been a dream, until my mother showed me the blood-soaked clothing, cut with the same precise lines I had seen them making that night.

Many years later, July 30, fate tested me again when I was airlifted to University Hospital in Colorado, fighting for my life and the life of my unborn son due to a rare pregnancy-related condition. Born at 32 weeks via emergency C-section, my newborn was what doctors call a 'feeder and grower,' needing time to gain strength before coming home, which was right around his due date, September 21. But the fear didn't end there. His first year was a blur of sleepless nights and terror with every breath he took.

These experiences didn't test me. They transformed me. They gave me insight, deeper than textbooks ever could, into what it means to live with trauma, and what it takes to heal from it. If you've felt stuck... If you've been afraid for so long it feels normal... If your trauma still echoes in your thoughts, your relationships, your body—you're not alone, and you're not beyond healing.

This book is for you.

Inside these pages, you'll find a blend of personal stories, professional insights, and practical tools – things I've used myself and still return to today. Whether you're a survivor, a seeker, or a mental health professional, this book is a resource you can come back to again and again.

Maybe you already know the shape of your pain. Maybe you're just beginning to name it. Maybe you're longing for healthier relationships or simply a deeper understanding of yourself. Wherever you are, this book will meet you there.

Healing, I've learned, isn't a straight climb. It's a winding trail, sometimes steep, sometimes gentle. Therapy helps, yes. But so does art, nature, breath, community, and mindfulness. I've written about creative healing before, a mindfulness coloring book called *Empowering Quotes from Iconic Women*. But *Power of HealingTrauma* goes deeper. It blends science with spirit. It's a guide, a companion, and a backpack filled with hope.

If you're a clinician, you'll find tools here.
If you're healing, you'll find validation.
If you're simply curious, you'll find clarity.
But most of all, I hope you find yourself. My deepest wish is that by the final page, you won't just see what trauma took, you'll see what healing can return.

Let's hike this trail together and discover what's around the next bend.
Take a deep, breath.
Your healing begins, now.

1

Digging Deep

Understanding the Science of Trauma

Think of a child who jumps at the sound of thunder, their heart racing, palms sweating, body frozen in place, and their whole body stiffens as if bracing for lightning to strike.

Now imagine that same startled feeling, but to the soft creak of a door, the unexpected tone of a phone, the soft touch of a loved one's hand.

This is what living with trauma feels like. The body's natural alarm system stays switched on, even after the storm has passed.

Trauma is not always loud. It doesn't leave visible scars or cast shadows others can see. Instead, it burrows deep settling into the body like frost into soil. It touches our thoughts, twists our emotions, and quietly shapes how we move through the world.

You may not realize how deep it's gone until it begins to show up in the quiet moments. In how your shoulders tense when someone raises their voice. In how hard it is to trust a kind word. In the way your stomach flips for no clear reason.

These aren't signs of weakness. These are signs your body is trying to protect you the only way it knows how. And that's where healing begins. Not in pushing these reactions away, but in learning how to listen to them.

Before we dive deeper, I want you to know this isn't a science textbook. You don't need a medical degree to understand your own body. But some knowledge is like sunlight for seeds: it helps grow what's buried beneath.

What is Trauma?

Trauma isn't just one thing. It's an entire experience. The impact is real and it runs deep.

This comprehensive definition is from experts at the American Psychological Association (APA), the Diagnostic and Statistical Manual 5 (DSM-5), and the Substance Abuse and Mental Health Services Administration (SAMHSA):

> Trauma is defined as an emotional and physical response to an event, series of events, or circumstances that involves actual or threatened death, serious injury, or violation. It can be experienced directly, witnessed, or learned about happening to someone close to you. The impact of trauma creates immediate responses like shock and denial, as well as long-term effects that can impact a person's mental, physical, social, emotional and spiritual well-being. These effects can include unpredictable emotions, flashbacks, strained relationships, and physical symptoms, fundamentally altering how a person functions in the world.

The Trauma-Informed Care Implementation Resource Center that is run by the Center for Health Care Strategies defines trauma as:

> Exposure to emotionally disturbing or

life-threatening events that affect well-being and functioning.

Trauma changes how we see the world. It shapes how we think, feel, connect, and function. It may leave you jumpy. Or foggy. Or so tired you feel like you're always swimming upstream.

It touches every layer of our being

- Mental: racing thoughts, brain fog, confusion
- Physical: chronic fatigue, tension, pain
- Emotional: numbness, mood swings, hopelessness
- Social: trust issues, isolation, fear of connection
- Spiritual: questioning purpose, meaning, or faith

These effects are all interconnected, creating a cycle that makes healing very complex, but very possible.

How Trauma Reshapes the Brain

Imagine your brain like a forest; lush, full of trails that guide how you feel and respond. When trauma hits, it's like a wildfire. It burns through certain areas, making old paths harder to find and reactive ones easier to take.

Trauma is about how our nervous system responds, how our body holds on to those experiences, and how our mind adapts. This all happens in ways we may not even be aware of.

Trauma disrupts the normal functioning of the brain in significant ways. Three key areas that are particularly affected:

- **The Amygdala (The Alarm System)** - Threat detector: making us feel hyperactive, constantly on edge, anxious, or reactive, jumping at sudden noises or feeling panicked in crowded spaces.
- **The Hippocampus (The Memory Keeper)** - Stores memories: fragmented memories, flashbacks, or diffi-

culty distinguishing past from present.

- **The Prefrontal Cortex (The Rational Mind)** – Regulate, reflect, and decide: harder to think clearly, manage emotions, and feel in control.

Neurotransmitter imbalances, particularly involving serotonin and dopamine, further complicate the picture. These chemical messengers play a role in mood regulation, and their imbalance can lead to symptoms of depression, anxiety, and even addiction as we seek ways to cope with the emotional turmoil.

The Body's Stress Response

The body's stress response is governed by the hypothalamic-pituitary-adrenal (HPA) axis. When we encounter a stressor, the HPA axis activates, releasing cortisol and other stress hormones. This system is designed to protect us by signaling danger and triggering necessary responses for survival.

In a healthy system, once the stressor is gone, the body returns to normal, and the stress response deactivates. However, when trauma remains unresolved, the stress response stays active, keeping the body in a prolonged state of alert. Eventually, the nervous system becomes overwhelmed, unable to regulate itself properly. Natural resources meant for healing and regeneration are instead spent managing ongoing stress, depleting essential energy reserves.

Healing requires restoring balance, allowing the body's stress response to deactivate and return to a regulated state. When the body's stress response remains continuously activated, it affects everything from immune function to digestion, often manifesting in a range of physical symptoms:

- **Chronic pain and headaches** often plague trauma survivors as the body's muscles remain tense and guarded.
- **Gastrointestinal problems** such as irritable bowel syndrome are common due to the gut-brain connection.
- **Sleep disturbances** become a nightly battle, robbing us of the restorative rest we need.

- **Our immune system** is also under attack, making us more susceptible to infections and illnesses.

This is our body's way of preparing for a fight-or-flight response. While this response is vital in the face of immediate danger, chronic activation due to unresolved trauma can lead to long-term health problems.

The Nervous System's Survival Responses

Our nervous system is designed for survival. It operates automatically, regulating functions like heart rate, breathing, digestion and reflexes.

Imagine walking alone at night and hearing footsteps rapidly approaching behind you. Your heart pounds, your muscles tighten, and your mind sharpens as you scan your surroundings. This is your fight or flight response at work, ensuring you are ready to react.

When we experience trauma, our bodies react instinctively through four core responses:

- **Fight:** We instinctively stand our ground. This may show up as snapping at a loved one who startles us, clenching our fists during a tense meeting, or feeling an overwhelming urge to defend ourselves even in safe situations.
- **Flight:** Our body urges us to escape, whether that means physically leaving a crowded store, avoiding confrontational conversations, or emotionally checking out during stressful moments.
- **Freeze:** Our system shuts down. We might find ourselves unable to speak during conflict, feeling stuck in our chair during a panic attack, or watching life pass by as if through a thick glass wall.
- **Fawn:** We attempt to pacify situations by becoming whatever others need us to be: apologizing when we've done nothing wrong, taking on extra work to avoid conflict, or neglecting our needs to keep others happy.

Trauma's Cellular Impact

Trauma doesn't just live in our mind. It settles in our body. Trauma goes deeper than thoughts. It can live in your posture, your breath, even your immune response.

The idea that our bodies remember what our minds try to forget is referred to as somatic memory. This powerful concept explains why trauma isn't just stored in our thoughts but becomes physically embedded in our being. Trauma imprints itself in our muscles, nervous system, and even in the way we carry ourselves each day.

That's why some people

- Hunch their shoulders without realizing it
- Breathe shallow
- Feel tension no massage can fully release

But here's the good news:

Healing can happen in the body, too.

These effects help explain why trauma is associated with increased risk for various health conditions, including cardiovascular disease, autoimmune disorders, and mental health issues. Fortunately, interventions like therapy, meditation, exercise, and social support can help mitigate some of these biological impacts.

Somatic therapies (body-based exercises, breath work, and trauma-informed movement) can help release trauma at the cellular level. Somatic therapy works with individuals to integrate and release these physical memories. Unlike traditional talk therapy that focuses primarily on cognitive processing, somatic approaches recognize that true healing must involve the body where trauma is stored.

Healing doesn't just involve changing your thoughts, it also means reconnecting with your body and teaching it how to feel safe again.

Research in the field of epigenetics has shown that trauma can alter gene expression, meaning that our body's response to stress can change at a cellular level. These changes don't just affect us; they can be passed down to future generations. This explains why some families experience generational cycles of anxiety, depression, and even physical illnesses linked to unresolved trauma.

The Gut-Brain Connection and Trauma

The relationship between your gut and your brain plays a crucial role in trauma responses. The gut is often referred to as the "second brain" because it contains millions of neurons that communicate directly with the brain via the vagus nerve.

This connection, known as the gut-brain axis, regulates mood, digestion, and immune function. When trauma occurs, it disrupts this communication, leading to digestive issues, inflammation, and emotional imbalances.

Trauma can alter the gut microbiome (the collection of bacteria in your intestines) which plays a significant role in mental health. When stress hormones flood the body, they can reduce the diversity of beneficial bacteria in the gut, increasing the risk of conditions like irritable bowel syndrome (IBS), anxiety, and depression.

Have you ever felt "butterflies" in your stomach when nervous? That's because the gut produces neurotransmitters like serotonin and dopamine, which regulate emotions. When the gut becomes dysregulated from trauma, it can lead to imbalances in these neurotransmitters, contributing to symptoms like chronic anxiety, digestive distress, and mood instability.

Healing the gut-brain connection involves a combination of dietary changes, mindfulness practices, and nervous system regulation techniques.

Here's a couple quick diet fixes that may assist with this journey:

1. Eat fermented foods like yogurt, kimchi, sauerkraut

2. Cut processed sugar

3. Eat anti-inflammatory nutrients (like Omega-3s)

It's not about a perfect diet, it's about supporting the systems that trauma dismantles.

Mind-Body Connection

If you've ever felt tired for no reason... or anxious over small things... or like joy was just out of reach...

That wasn't your fault. It was your nervous system asking for care.

Healing starts when we stop blaming ourselves and start listening to what our body's been trying to say. These sensations are not random. This is our body's way of managing unresolved emotional pain. Here's how stress can manifest physically:

- Tension headaches
- Anxiety or flutters in our stomach
- Weakened immune system
- Overactive or inactive digestion

Imagine your nervous system as a garden that's been trampled. With proper care, new pathways can grow, like tender shoots pushing through disturbed soil. Old trauma responses can be gently pruned back, making room for more adaptive patterns to flourish.

The process of healing may include learning to recognize your body's signals which involves building a relationship with your body's wisdom.

Throughout the following chapters, we will explore practical exercises designed to strengthen the mind-body connection, regulate stress responses, and promote healing. Each practice is another step in reclaiming your inner landscape, setting you up for long-term success in your healing journey.

Understanding trauma's impact on our biology isn't just about knowledge, it's about recognizing our body's innate capacity for healing and resilience.

Like a river finding new paths after a flood, our systems naturally seek balance and restoration.

The good news is, just as trauma changed us, so too can recovery reshape our path forward; leading us back to a place of greater peace and connection with ourselves.

The Brain's Capacity for Change

While trauma leaves profound imprints on our brain and body, here's a remarkable truth that offers hope: our brains possess an extraordinary ability to change and heal. This capacity, known as neuroplasticity, means that the same brain that was rewired by trauma can be rewired again through healing.

The memories and emotions that feel so overwhelming now can be processed and integrated in new ways. The nervous system that learned to stay on high alert can rest again. The body that holds trauma's tension can release it.

Recap

Trauma is a complex experience that affects the mind, body, and soul. It alters how we perceive and respond to the world, disrupting mental clarity, physical health, emotional balance, and social connections. It can live in your thoughts, your breath, your relationships, and the way your body tenses when no one is looking. Those changes are real, not imagined. But we've also discovered something powerful: what was rewired by trauma can be rewired through healing.

In the Next Chapter

In Seeds of Change, we'll explore how healing actually works inside the brain. You'll learn how thoughts, habits, and emotions are shaped through neuroplasticity and how small, repeated actions can build new pathways toward peace, connection, and resilience. Our brain and body are not permanently damaged by trauma, they are just waiting for the right conditions to restore balance. This chapter is about hope, not the wishful kind, but the kind that grows roots, so even when you can't feel a shift, know that something is happening beneath the surface.

2

Seeds of Change

Neuroplasticity, Memory and Emotions

Imagine you've always taken the same well-worn path to the river. It's easy to walk, the grass is flattened, and the rocks are smooth from years of use. It's become second nature to you, and you don't even have to think about where to step.

One day, you decide to try a different path. A path that isn't as clear, where the grass is taller, and the ground feels more unlevel and unfamiliar.

At first, it's difficult. You stumble, and it feels like the new route will never feel as comfortable as the old one. But, as you keep walking this new path, something begins to change. The grass starts to bend under your feet, the ground softens, and a trail begins to form

Overtime, what once felt awkward and difficult becomes easier, until one day, the new path feels just as natural as the old one.

This is a perfect example of neuroplasticity.

When you choose to create a new path, whether in your thinking, behavior, or coping skills, your brain begins to form new neural connections. The more you walk down this new path, the stronger those connections become, until they are just as natural and automatic as the old ones. Each step plants seeds of change in your neural connections that, with attention and care, grow into new patterns of thinking and being.

This proves the power of our brains. It shows that change, though initially very challenging, becomes easier the more we practice and commit to it. Transformation is always there, waiting for us to make the first move.

Neuroplasticity

Neuroplasticity is an awe-inspiring concept that reveals the brain's ability to change and adapt. Our brains are not fixed; they are ever-evolving, continuously forming new connections and pathways. This dynamic nature is particularly relevant in trauma recovery, as it highlights the brain's capacity to rewire itself, allowing us to heal and create new thought patterns, behavior patterns, and emotional responses.

Imagine your brain as a dense forest. Every thought or behavior creates a pathway through the trees. The more often you travel along a particular path, the clearer and more established it becomes. In the same way, when you consciously engage in new, healthier habits, you're forging fresh neural pathways that gradually replace the older, maladaptive ones formed by trauma.

Through consistent practice, these new connections allow you to shift away from the patterns of distress that once felt inescapable. This remarkable adaptability of the brain was once considered limited after childhood. However, research over the past several decades has shattered that myth, showing that our brains retain the ability to grow and change throughout our entire life.

This discovery has opened new possibilities for trauma recovery, empowering individuals to rewire their brains by practicing new, healing behaviors.

In trauma recovery, the brain's ability to form new connections means you can overwrite the negative thought patterns, emotional dysregulation, and heightened anxiety often created by trauma.

Neuroplasticity offers hope by showing that you can reshape the way you process emotions and experiences, fostering healthier thought patterns and more adaptive responses to stress.

Consider the case of Jane, a trauma survivor who struggled with persistent anxiety and intrusive thoughts. Through regular mindfulness practice, Jane learned to observe her thoughts without judgment, allowing her to create a mental space where she could respond rather than react. Over time, this simple practice led to meaningful changes in the brain, ultimately improving her emotional regulation and helping her manage stress more effectively. Jane's journey is a testament to the transformative potential that neuroplasticity offers.

Harnessing Neuroplasticity for Trauma Recovery

When you understand the powerful role of neuroplasticity in healing, it becomes clear that recovery is not only possible but within our control. By engaging in practices that stimulate our brain's ability to rewire itself, we can actively shift the way we process traumatic memories and emotional responses. These practices can include:

- **Mindfulness meditation**
  This practice enhances awareness, helping to observe thoughts without judgment and rewire the brain's stress response.

- **Cognitive Behavioral Therapy (CBT)**
  Focuses on identifying and challenging negative thought patterns that contribute to emotional distress, helping to reshape neural pathways and foster healthier ways of thinking.

- **Learning new skills**
  Whether it's picking up a new hobby such as learning to play an instrument, or learning how to paint, these activities stimulate neuroplasticity by creating fresh neural connections.

By consistently engaging in healing practices, we can build new neural pathways that enable healthier emotional regulation and resilience. In turn, these new pathways gradually replace the old patterns of fear and anxiety created by trauma, shaping a more balanced emotional landscape.

The Role of Memory in Trauma

Trauma not only leaves an emotional imprint but also deeply impacts how our brains store and recall memories. There are two types of memory that are especially affected: explicit and implicit memory.

- **Explicit memory** refers to the conscious recall of facts and events, like remembering a vacation or your first day of school.
- **Implicit memory** involves unconscious recall, such as remembering how to ride a bike or experiencing the emotional undertone of an event.

Trauma distorts these memory systems, often fragmenting memories into intrusive, disconnected pieces. You might suddenly experience vivid, disjointed images or sensations related to a traumatic event, and these memories can surface without warning, disrupting daily life.

Additionally, trauma can make it difficult to recall the specifics of an event clearly, leaving you with a sense of confusion or frustration.

Flashbacks are another common manifestation of trauma's impact on memory. These vivid, distressing recollections often feel as if the traumatic event is occurring all over again.

Flashbacks can be triggered by certain sights, sounds, smells, or other stimuli that remind us of past trauma. For example, the scent of a certain perfume or cologne may send you back to an unpleasant encounter. In these moments, the amygdala (your brain's fear center) becomes overactive, triggering a cascade of stress hormones and causing your body to relive trauma.

Flashbacks aren't just mental; they can engage our entire sensory system, creating a full-bodied, overwhelming experience.

Emotional Numbness
Why Trauma Makes Us Feel Disconnected

Imagine living life behind a thick, foggy glass; you can see the world, but you can't fully engage with it. Living with trauma is similar to living behind the foggy glass. Often, emotional numbness marks our state of being, as trauma leaves us feeling disconnected to our daily life.

Trauma symptoms can also include a pervasive sense of emptiness and difficulty experiencing joy or sadness. You might find yourself going through the motions and performing tasks without any sense of fulfillment or emotion.

Emotional numbness is a state of being where you feel detached from your emotions. This numbness often manifests in trauma survivors to help cope with overwhelming experiences.

The causes of emotional numbness are rooted in various mechanisms that your mind and body employ to protect you. This response is not just psychological but deeply physiological, affecting your entire being. Over time, it can become a significant barrier to experiencing the full spectrum of human emotions.

Avoidance and dissociation are two primary strategies of emotional numbness:

- **Avoidance** involves steering clear of situations, people, or activities that might trigger painful memories. For instance, you might avoid social gatherings because they remind you of the connections you lost or the trauma you experienced.

- **Dissociation,** on the other hand, is a psychological response where you disconnect from reality. It can range from feeling disconnected from your surroundings to more severe forms like depersonalization, where you might feel detached from your own body or sense of self.

When you're exposed to prolonged stress, your body remains in a constant state of alertness, making it difficult to relax or feel safe. This chronic state of hyper-arousal can lead to emotional exhaustion, where your mind shuts down its emotional responses to conserve energy. Over time, this can become a default way of coping, leading to persistent emotional numbness.

Reconnecting with your emotions is a gradual process that requires patience and compassion. Gradual exposure to emotions is a crucial step. Start by allowing yourself to feel small, manageable emotions. For instance, watch a movie that evokes mild emotions and notice how you feel. Writing down these feelings in a journal adds benefit. This practice can help you become more comfortable with experiencing emotions without feeling overwhelmed.

Self-compassion is paramount in this process. You can practice compassionate self-talk by acknowledging your struggles and offering yourself words of kindness. This is not about forcing emotions but gently inviting them back into your life, allowing you to experience the richness of human emotion once again.

Remember: emotional numbness is a complex but understandable response to trauma. It serves as a protective mechanism but can hinder your ability to live fully. By understanding its causes and employing strategies to reconnect with your emotions, you can begin to thaw that emotional frost.

Rewiring the Brain to Heal and Manage Trauma

Neuroplasticity offers a profound message of hope: the brain is capable of change, growth, and healing at any stage of life. Trauma may reshape neural pathways, but it does not define them permanently.

By consciously engaging in practices that support neuroplasticity, such as mindfulness (present moment thinking), cognitive restructuring (reframe negative thought patterns), and talk therapy, you can actively rewire your brain to process emotions more effectively and form healthier patterns of thinking and behavior.

Recap

Trauma can create emotional numbness or dysregulation, but neuroplasticity allows us to rebuild our emotional resilience. With consistent effort and the right tools, we can reclaim our mind, our emotions, and our sense of self, stepping forward with greater empowerment and peace.

So far, we have learned how trauma often manifests in ways that can be mistaken for other conditions or even dismissed as common ailments. By practicing the coping skills you will learn in the coming chapters, you can train your brain to feel safe in the present rather than trapped in the past.

In the Next Chapter

Next, we will learn how to recognize trauma. We'll explore self-screening approaches that go beyond the obvious signs, examining both psychological and physiological indicators that signal unresolved trauma. We will also learn to identify trauma responses that might otherwise be misinterpreted or overlooked.

Let's keep moving.

3

Eye of the Storm

Recognizing and Screening Trauma

All I heard was the sterile hum of a hospital room, the constant beeping of machines tracking every heartbeat, every breath. The rhythmic sounds became both a comfort and a torment; a reassurance that my baby boy was still alive, yet a reminder of how delicate his life remained.

I stood in the Neonatal Intensive Care Unit (NICU), buried under the crushing weight of fear, disoriented by the sudden darkness that had descended upon what should have been a joyful time. My son, born nearly two months premature on July 30 instead of his September 21 due date, lay fighting for his life, whileI fought my own battles against fear and my body's rebellion.

I remember the day perfectly. Thunder had been crashing across the mountains since dawn, the sky dark with a vengeance. Helicopter blades fighting the wind as I lay strapped inside, medications flooding my veins. As we climbed through the storm's fury, something remarkable happened; suddenly we broke through the thunderclouds into an expanse of pristine blue sky, stretching endlessly toward Denver.

The transition was so absolute, so perfect, it seemed impossible, as if some divine hand had swept the heavens clear, carving out a path just for us. Despite the drugs clouding my thoughts, despite my terror and pain, I felt my lips curve into a smile. In that suspended moment between earth and sky, between life and death, I found something I desperately needed. Hope.

Each moment after was engulfed in uncertainty and a helplessness I never thought I'd experience.

Days blurred together. The stress settled into my body like an unwelcome guest, lingering long after the immediate crisis had passed. I told myself I was fine, that I just needed time, but the nights betrayed me. I'd wake up gasping for air, drenched in sweat, heart pounding, convinced "they" were coming to take me, away, further from my baby.

These nightmares—vivid delusions that felt terrifyingly real—left me afraid to sleep. I oscillated between these paranoid fears and the very real anguish that my premature son wouldn't survive. No matter how much I tried to push through, the tension never lifted. I felt trapped. My chest stayed tight, my sleep was restless, and the smallest triggers sent my heart racing.

Eventually, the emotional strain became too much. Sitting in my doctor's office, I listened as they handed me a prescription for anti-anxiety medication. I stared at the bottle in my hand, feeling a mix of relief and defeat.

This wasn't the plan. This wasn't supposed to happen. But it did.

In that moment, I realized how completely I had been suffocated by this trauma. The emergency delivery, the helicopter ride out of the storm, the medications that saved my life while leaving me disoriented, the separation from my child after being in utero for 7 months. Even though we had survived it all, I felt confined to the eye of the storm.

At this point in my life, I didn't have any survival skills for coping. But by becoming aware of it, and naming it, something shifted. I no longer allowed it to have the power to consume me. Acknowledging that I needed help was both humbling and empowering. It was the first step in understanding that trauma doesn't just leave when the crisis ends. It stays, entrenched in daily life, manifesting in nightmares, in paranoia, in the constant fear of loss.

It was taking a major toll on me, and even though I didn’t have the equipment for digging through something of this magnitude, I knew I had to get myself out. A path gradually started to clear, and I dug my way out one step closer to the surface, one step closer to the light.

Recognizing Trauma

As we've discovered, trauma can manifest in various forms. Whether it's a result of a specific event or an accumulation of stress over time, it may show up as emotional numbness, anxiety, or physical tension that lingers long after the initial experience.

By acknowledging the impact these events you can begin to understand how trauma managed to shape our thoughts, emotions, and behaviors.

Remember, the recognition of trauma isn't about reliving the pain, but rather about identifying the ways it now affects your life. This allows us to know exactly what we are dealing with because the first step to change is always awareness.

Why This Matters

Self-assessment gives us the power to recognize our own needs, limitations, and potential areas of growth. By bringing awareness to any patterns, we can begin our healing journey more empowered and better informed.

One of the most important aspects of self-assessing trauma is to approach it with compassion. Trauma often comes with self-blame, confusion, or denial. However, in this chapter, you are encouraged to become an observer of your own experiences **without** judgment.

A Note Before Beginning Your Self-Assessment
As you prepare to explore trauma responses through self-assessment, it's important to create a safe and supportive environment for this part of the journey. Self-assessment can bring up unexpected emotions and memories, even if uncomfortable, this is perfectly normal.

Here are a few basic coping mechanisms to consider before we begin:

- **Create a Safe Space:** Choose a quiet, private location where you feel secure and won't be interrupted.
- **Set Boundaries:** Decide in advance how much time you'll spend on these exercises and honor your limits.
- **Promote Comfort:** Have comforting items nearby like a warm blanket, soothing tea, or calming music.
- **Know Your Support System:** trusted friends or family, therapist or counselor, crisis hotlines (keep these numbers handy), online support groups.
- **Listen to Your Body:** If you feel overwhelmed, take breaks. You can always return to these exercises later.
- **Practice Grounding:** Before and after these exercises, use simple grounding techniques like deep breathing or feeling your feet on the floor.

Signs and Symptoms

Trauma is complex and affects individuals in different ways. Below are some common signs and symptoms that trauma may be influencing your life:

1. **Emotional Symptoms:**
    - Feelings of sadness, hopelessness, or numbness
    - Anger or irritability without a clear cause
    - Anxiety or constant worry, even when situations don't call for it
    - Emotional detachment or difficulty connecting with others
    - Frequent mood swings
2. **Cognitive Symptoms:**

- Intrusive thoughts or memories of traumatic events
- Difficulty concentrating or making decisions
- Negative thoughts about yourself or the world
- Memory issues or blocks related to specific events
- Disassociation or feeling disconnected from your body or surroundings

3. **Physical Symptoms:**
   - Fatigue or low energy levels
   - Sleep disturbances (insomnia, nightmares)
   - Chronic pain, headaches, or muscle tension
   - Digestive issues or appetite changes
   - Increased startle response or hyper-vigilance (always being on edge)
4. **Behavioral Symptoms:**
   - Avoiding places, people, or activities that remind you of trauma
   - Increased use of substances (alcohol, drugs) to cope
   - Difficulty maintaining relationships or withdrawing from loved ones
   - Procrastination or feeling unable to complete tasks
   - Engaging in risky or self-destructive behaviors

Self-Assessment

The following exercises and questions will help you assess whether past trauma is influencing your current state of well-being.

Remember, self-assessment is a tool for self-awareness, **NOT** *self-judgment. Approach each question with curiosity and openness.*

Emotional Check-In

- How do I feel emotionally on most days? Am I generally calm, anxious, or overwhelmed?
- Do I frequently feel sadness or hopelessness without understanding why?
- Are there emotions I tend to suppress or avoid?

Cognitive Reflection

- Do I often have thoughts that spiral into negativity or self-criticism?
- Do I feel stuck thinking about past events that cause distress?
- Have I noticed any changes in my memory or ability to focus?

Physical Body Awareness

- How does my body feel daily? Do I often feel tense or tired?
- Have I experienced any chronic pain or physical ailments that don't seem to have a medical cause?
- Do I struggle with sleep, either with falling asleep, staying asleep, or having distressing dreams?

Behavioral Patterns

- Am I avoiding any activities, people, or places because they make me feel uncomfortable or unsafe?
- Have I noticed any changes in my relationships? Am I

more withdrawn, distant, or irritable with those I love?

- Am I engaging in coping mechanisms that are unhealthy, such as drinking, overeating, or other self-destructive behaviors?

Trauma Screening Tools

While personal reflection is important, formal trauma screening tools can help you gain a deeper understanding of your experiences.

Below are additional screenings that can be found online. Consider using one or more of the following tools to broaden your assessment and build your self-knowledge.

The Post-Traumatic Stress Disorder (PTSD) Checklist (PCL-5)
This is a widely used self-report measure for PTSD. It helps individuals identify common PTSD symptoms, such as intrusive thoughts, avoidance behaviors, and hyper-arousal. This tool can be particularly useful if you have experienced specific traumatic events like accidents, natural disasters, or violence.

The Trauma Symptom Checklist-40 (TSC-40)
This tool assesses a range of trauma-related symptoms including depression, dissociation, and sleep disturbances. The TSC-40 offers a broader look at how trauma affects your day-to-day life.

The Adverse Childhood Experiences (ACE) Questionnaire
This 10-question survey focuses on childhood trauma and its long-term impact. Childhood trauma often has profound effects on adult mental and physical health. The ACE questionnaire can help illuminate how early experiences may still be influencing your life today.

Reflecting on Your Results

Once you've completed the self-assessment and any screening tools, it's time to reflect.

We strongly recommend journaling results. You may find that certain questions brought up emotions or memories you weren't expecting. Remember, the goal of this chapter is to raise awareness, not to overwhelm or re-traumatize you.

Key Reflections

- Patterns: Are there recurring patterns or themes in your emotional, cognitive, or behavioral responses?
- Severity: How often do you experience these symptoms? Are they occasional or persistent?
- Triggers: Can you identify specific triggers for your responses? Are there situations, people, or places that intensify your feelings or reactions?

Try to identify any subtle and overlooked signs as hidden trauma is like a shadow lurking in the background of your mind, subtly influencing your thoughts, emotions, and behaviors without making its presence overtly known.

Unlike obvious trauma, which is often linked to significant, identifiable events, hidden trauma stems from experiences that might not seem painful on the surface but have left a lasting impact. These experiences can include chronic emotional neglect, subtle forms of abuse, or prolonged periods of stress. Because these events do not fit the conventional definition of trauma, they are often overlooked, both by individuals and professionals. However, their effects can be just as profound, quietly shaping your life in ways you might not immediately recognize. One of the most insidious aspects of hidden trauma is that its signs are often subtle and easily ignored.

Chronic feelings of emptiness can be a significant indicator of unresolved trauma. You might go through your day feeling like something is missing, a void that you can't quite fill no matter what activities or accomplishments you pursue. This pervasive sense of emptiness can lead to a lack of motivation and a feeling of being disconnected from life.

Difficulty concentrating or staying focused is another sign. You might find your mind wandering during important tasks or struggle to retain information. This can affect your performance at work or school, leading to frustration and self-doubt.

Persistent fatigue that cannot be explained by medical conditions is also a common symptom of hidden trauma. You might wake up feeling exhausted, no matter how much sleep you get. This fatigue can sap your energy and make it difficult to engage in daily activities, leaving you feeling drained and overwhelmed.

These are all subtle signs that your body is signaling something deeper is at play, and it's crucial to pay attention to them.

Structured Journaling Practice

Additional journaling can be a powerful tool for uncovering and processing trauma, but it's important to approach it mindfully. Remember, you don't need to share your journal with anyone. This is your private space for exploration and expression.

If journaling brings up intense emotions or memories, honor those feelings while maintaining your safety. Consider sharing significant insights with your therapist or counselor if you're working with one.

Things to keep in mind:

- Start with "lighter" topics and gradually explore deeper as you feel ready
- If memories or emotions become overwhelming, pause and use grounding techniques
- Focus on sensations and feelings rather than detailed traumatic narratives
- End each session with a positive reflection or self-compassionate statement
- If difficult material surfaces, reach out to your support system

When you are ready to begin, here's a structured approach to trauma-informed journaling.

Set Up Your Practice

- Choose a private, secure place to keep your journal
- Set aside 15-20 minutes for writing each day
- Begin with a grounding exercise
- Keep tissues and water nearby

Prompting Questions for Exploration

- **Body Awareness**
  Where do I feel tension in my body today? What physical sensations arise when I think about challenging situations? How has my energy level been today?
- **Emotional Landscape**
  What emotions am I experiencing most frequently? Are there any emotions I find difficult to express? What triggers a strong emotional response?
- **Pattern Recognition**
  What situations make me feel unsafe? Do I notice any recurring themes in my relationships? What coping mechanisms (call support, listening to your body, practicing grounding) do I use when stressed?

Recap

Recognizing and addressing hidden trauma can be a transformative experience, allowing you to understand the deeper layers of your emotional and psychological environment. By paying attention to subtle signs, engaging in reflective practices, and seeking professional guidance, you can uncover the hidden sources of your distress and take meaningful steps toward healing.

This process is not just about identifying trauma but also about reclaiming your sense of self and well-being, paving the way for a more balanced and fulfilling life.

In the Next Chapter

In the next chapter, we will explore the power of grounding techniques and how they can help center your energy. We will also guide you through clearing sacred spaces and creating an environment where healing can truly take root.

Professional Disclosure

While self-exploration is essential, professional guidance is equally important in uncovering and addressing hidden trauma. Trauma-informed therapy can provide the support and expertise needed to navigate this complex process.

If you recognize significant trauma-related patterns or symptoms, know that you're not alone, and there is help available.

Professional support, such as a therapist, intuitive energy healer, or spiritual coach can offer guidance on how to work through trauma effectively.

A trauma-informed therapist understands the nuanced ways trauma can manifest and can offer tailored strategies to help you uncover and heal from trauma. They can guide you through therapeutic techniques such as Eye-Movement Desensitization and Reprocessing (EMDR), Brain Spotting, or Somatic Experiencing, which are designed to address trauma on a deep, subconscious level.

Holistic practices that we will talk about in the coming chapters will help you regain control over your mind and body and can be practiced with or without professional therapy, but never hesitate to call for help.

4

Back on Solid Ground

Grounding and Clearing Sacred Space

So far we've seen how transformation often emerges from our deepest wounds. But sometimes, those wounds don't just heal; they break us open in ways we never expected, leading us toward a spiritual awakening through our darkest moments.

This is where my own path took an unexpected turn.

My father, known to most as '*Moondog*', was my lighthouse. At 6'3" and over 250 pounds for most of his years, he was a towering presence—solid, protective, immovable. Yet beneath that strength was a gentleness as soft as a wish whispered to a dandelion.

A Vietnam veteran left disabled by Agent Orange; he carried his burdens with grace, meeting life with arms wide open until the very end.

His laughter could fill a room and his wisdom shaped my every decision. He had a gift for finding light in the darkest places, teaching me that joy could exist alongside the pain.

"*Everything will be okay*," he'd say, and because it was him saying it, I would believe it.

Even when his body failed him, when walking and talking became impossible, his eyes still held that mischievous flicker that said, "*Watch this...*"—a promise that something unexpectedly hilarious was about to unfold.

I thought I was prepared for his death. I told myself that watching him suffer was worse than anything that could follow.

I was wrong.

When the heart monitor flatlined and the nurses rushed in, it wasn't just his heart that stopped, it was as if the world itself lost its center of gravity. In the aftermath of his passing, I found myself grasping for solid ground in a world that suddenly felt too vast and too empty. In that vulnerable space, I realized grounding is not just a practice. It's a lifeline.

When trauma shatters your foundation, when grief leaves you untethered, when a spiritual awakening cracks you open; you need ways to return to yourself, to feel your feet back on solid ground.

This chapter is about that return. These practices teach you to hold grief and joy, loss and love, past and present, in the same breath.

Whether you're navigating acute trauma, chronic stress, or the profound shifts that come with healing, these skills will keep you connected to your body, your breath, and your life. They offer a stable foundation where healing becomes not just possible, but inescapable.

Many take mere seconds to implement, bringing you back to yourself when you need it most. It is here that the genuine process of healing emerges. Let's dive in.

Grounding

Have you ever felt like you're floating away from yourself? Like the world becomes distant, dreamlike, as if you're watching it pass by? Your body might feel strange, too light or too heavy, not quite real. Sounds seem to come from far away, and time itself feels distorted.

In these moments, you're caught between past and present, between here and somewhere else.

Or perhaps it's the opposite and everything feels too close, too intense? Your heart races, your thoughts spiral, and the past crashes into the present with overwhelming force. Memories and sensations flood in without warning, making it hard to remember that you're safe, that you're here, that what you're reliving isn't happening right now.

These experiences are common responses to trauma. Your nervous system, while it is trying to protect you, sometimes disconnects from the present moment or becomes hyper-alert to potential threats. It's not your fault; it's your brain doing what it learned to do to keep you safe. But you don't have to remain caught in this hyper-vigilant state.

Grounding is a practical technique for reestablishing awareness of the present moment. It involves deliberately shifting attention to your immediate physical surroundings and bodily sensations when overwhelmed by difficult emotions or intrusive thoughts. This practice helps deactivate the stress response, allowing you to regain mental clarity and emotional balance by connecting with what is real and tangible in the here and now.

The power of creating sacred spaces is the foundation of this journey.

When my father passed, I felt an instinctive need to clear a space for him, not just physically but energetically. It was about making room for healing, for remembrance, for the presence of something beyond loss. In that space, I surrounded myself with objects that connected us, things that carried his essence and brought a sense of peace. A necklace of his, a quiet reminder of his love. A soft, calming throw blanket that invited me to rest when grief felt overwhelming. I placed plants beside his picture, their quiet growth mirroring my own slow process of healing. His ashes, held in a metal heart, rested among them. These small, intentional acts became a form of grounding, teaching me that healing isn't only an internal process; it is also shaped by the energy of the spaces we create. In crafting a sanctuary of peace and connection, I found a way to hold my grief with tenderness, allowing both loss and love to exist side by side.

Your environment has a profound impact on your nervous system and just as trauma can leave energetic imprints in your body, spaces can hold energies that affect your well-being.

Creating safe, nurturing spaces (both in your physical environment and in your mind) is an essential part of grounding and beginning to authentic healing.

Your Physical Sanctuary

Think of your living space as an extension of your healing journey. Each room, each corner, carries its own energy. When spaces are cluttered or chaotic, that energy can feel stuck, heavy, like a weight pressing against your spirit. But when you mindfully create order and beauty, your space becomes a container for healing.

Start with one small area, perhaps a corner of your bedroom or a spot by a window. Clear away anything that doesn't serve your healing: objects that trigger difficult memories, Items that create visual noise, things that are broken or damaged, clutter that makes you feel heavy or anxious.

As you clear the space, you're not just organizing, you're creating energetic breathing room. Notice how different the space feels as it opens up.

Now, thoughtfully add elements that support grounding and peace. Try things like:

- Natural materials like wood, stone, or plants
- Soft, comfortable textures
- Calming colors that soothe your nervous system
- Objects that carry positive memories or meanings
- Elements that engage your senses in pleasant ways

This is like clearing a path for fresh energy to flow. You can also try adding a few items that bring you strength. For me it is a few things that remind me of my dad, a wall mount (I made for him years ago) that continues to dry wet, snowy clothes at the end of a long day.

You can actively raise the vibration of your own environment with a few intentional practices. To cleanse your energy try opening windows to let fresh air circulate, ring a bell or singing bowl to move stagnant energy, burn sage, palo santo, or incense (if you enjoy these scents), use salt lamps or crystals that resonate with you and/or play uplifting music or nature sounds.

Next, try creating flow by arranging furniture to allow easy movement and position things to face natural light when possible. Create clear pathways through rooms, balancing different elements (soft and firm, light and dark) to create flow, and include living plants to bring in vital energy.

Now that our surroundings are ready, let's talk more about our inner landscape because the sanctuary you create in your mind is just as important as your physical space.

Your Inner Sanctuary

This is a place you can return to whenever you need to ground yourself, regardless of where you are physically. Let's begin by imagining a place where you feel completely safe and at peace. It could be:

- A sun-warmed beach with gentle waves
- A cozy cabin in the woods
- A magical garden filled with flowers
- A room filled with soft light and comfort

Any place that feels secure and nurturing to you. Take time to develop this space in rich imaginative detail:

- What does it look like in different lights?
- What gentle sounds are present?
- What comforting scents fill the air?
- What textures can you feel?

- What is the temperature like?

The more you visit and develop the inner sanctuary of your mind, the stronger its grounding power becomes. It will eventually be the most reliable refuge you now have access to at anytime.

Similar to your physical space, you can raise your personal vibration as well. Keep in mind, grounding isn't just about coming back to your body; it's about harmonizing your energy with higher frequencies of healing and peace. Some ways you can elevate your personal vibration while staying grounded are through breath, through movement, or through intention.

The Role of Breath in Grounding

A powerful grounding practice I use is conscious breathing. We will go more in detail on breathing in the coming chapters but when I struggle with moments of anxiety, where it feels like the world is spinning out of control, I focus on my breath, taking slow, deep breaths, as I feel the air filling my lungs, and I release the tension with each exhale. It's a simple practice, but it's one that has made a huge difference in how I manage stress.

Breathing helps me reconnect with the present moment, especially when I'm caught between the past and the present. When I would feel the weight of grief or unresolved emotions pushing me into memories I couldn't control, I'd breathe through it. I'd picture my breath as a tool to keep me grounded. I'd imagine the inhale pulling me into the present moment and the exhale releasing the past. With each breath, I feel a little lighter, a little more connected to myself and to the world around me.

Below are some examples of how to raise your personal vibration:

Through Breath

- Ocean breath (ujjayi) for strength and presence
- Heart-opening breaths that lift your energy
- Humming or toning to raise vibration through sound

- Dragon breaths to release stagnant energy
- Circular breathing to create flow

Through Movement

- Gentle stretching that opens energy channels
- Walking barefoot on natural ground
- Dancing freely to uplifting music
- Yoga poses that make you feel strong and centered
- Any movement that helps you feel both energized and grounded

Through Intention

- Setting daily intentions for peace and healing
- Creating morning or evening rituals
- Speaking affirmations that resonate with your truth
- Visualizing yourself surrounded by healing light
- Connecting with gratitude
- Energy Clearing Practices

Learning to clear and protect your energy is an essential grounding skill. Just as we shower each day to cleanse our physical body, our energy field requires regular clearing to maintain its strength and clarity and ensure that your nervous system functions optimally.

Just like your body can become physically fatigued when it's carrying too much stress or tension, your energy field can become weighed down by unresolved emotions, negative experiences, or the energies of others. When this happens, your nervous system may become overstimulated or sluggish, making it harder for you to feel balanced, present, and at peace.

These grounding techniques can help you through overstimulation.

5-4-3-2-1 Sensory Awareness Exercise

- **See – 5**
  Identify 5 things you can see
  Look around and name them out loud or in your mind. It could be the colors of the walls, the pattern on a rug, or the leaves rustling outside your window.

- **Touch – 4**
  Find 4 things you can touch
  Feel for texture, temperature, and weight. Feel the heat from the lights, the smoothness of a table, or the weight of a cushion.

- **Hear – 3**
  Listen for 3 distinct sounds
  Focus on each one for a moment. It might be the hum of an air conditioner, birds chirping, or distant traffic.

- **Smell – 2**
  Identify 2 scents in your environment
  Take a deep breath and notice them. This could be the aroma of coffee or the fresh air.

- **Taste – 1**
  Focus on 1 thing you can taste
  It might be subtle but pay attention to it. It might be the lingering flavor of a meal.

Physical Grounding
Grounding through physical touch is another simple yet powerful technique. When you feel overwhelmed, hold an object that has a reassuring texture, such as a stress ball, a smooth stone, or a piece of fabric. Focus on the sensations in your hand, the weight, the temperature, and the texture.

This tactile focus can help divert your attention from distressing thoughts and provide a sense of comfort.

You might also try pressing your feet firmly against the ground, feeling the solid support beneath you. This physical connection can reinforce your sense of stability and presence.

Daily Cleansing Rituals

Creating a daily cleansing ritual helps release accumulated stress, negative energy, and emotions that aren't yours to carry. Think of it as energetic hygiene; a way to start fresh each day and clear away the residue of whatever you've encountered.

Start your day by creating sacred space for yourself.

A great example would be when you awake before checking your phone or engaging with the world.

- Take three deep breaths to center yourself
- Feel your body awakening and becoming present
- Surround yourself with golden or white light*
- Speak aloud an affirmation of protection such as "*I know I am protected*"*
- Set boundaries/limits for the day ahead such as limiting social media to 30 mins per day*

Then, as you get out of bed and prepare for the day; carry or wear objects that help you feel protected (crystals, meaningful jewelry, etc). This will set your day off feeling protected and allow for positive energy to flow.

** These are referred to as protection setting when done together*

At the end of your day clear away whatever energy you've accumulated by:

- Removing shoes and any constricting clothing
- Shake out your limbs to release stuck energy
- Take a few deep sighs to let go of the day
- If possible, step outside briefly to connect with fresh air

Next, sit quietly for a few moments:

- Place one hand on your heart

- Thank yourself for making it through another day
- Release any judgments about what may have happened
- Set an intention for peaceful rest by mentally stating something like: "I will sleep peacefully and protected."

Then lay down and embrace the restfulness that takes over your body as your drift asleep. If there is any delay; take this time to mentally list a few things you are grateful for. This daily cleansing ritual will set you up for the healing journey.

At times when you need to clear energy in the moment, here are a few quick techniques:

The Energy Shake

- Stand with feet planted firmly
- Shake your whole body for 30 seconds
- Focus especially on hands and feet
- End with three deep breaths

Quick Cord Cutting

- Visualize any cords connecting you to difficult situations
- Use light (or scissors of light) to gently cut these cords
- Send the energy back to its source with love
- Seal your energy field afterward

Window of Tolerance

Pay attention to your window of tolerance, which is the zone where you can effectively process experiences without becoming overwhelmed or shut down. This refers to your mental head space. Signs you're outside your window include: feeling hyper-aroused (anxious, panicky, racing thoughts), feeling hypo-aroused (numb, disconnected, foggy), physical symptoms like rapid heartbeat or feeling frozen. When you notice these signs, use grounding techniques to help regulate your nervous system.

Grounding for Support

Grounding is both your emergency rescue plan and your long-term foundation for healing. By creating spaces that support you, keeping your energy field clear, and having a few reliable grounding techniques in your back pocket, you're building yourself a solid launching pad for an incredible healing journey. And remember, raising your vibration doesn't mean floating off into space. True healing happens when you can stay connected to the earth while reaching for the light.

In my own personal experience after the passing of my dad, I felt lost, adrift in grief. I couldn't shake the heaviness in my heart, and it felt like the world around me was moving in slow motion. One afternoon, I decided to go for a hike, an old habit that always helped me feel more grounded. As I walked, I focused on the sensation of my feet on the earth. I could feel the firmness of the ground beneath me, the gentle breeze on my skin, and the scent of pine in the air. With each step, I imagined my grief being absorbed by the earth, grounding me and helping me release what I couldn't carry any longer. I paid attention to the sounds of the snow crunching under my feet, and the soft whirling of the wind. By the time I returned home, I felt a deep sense of peace and connection. Nature, in its stillness and beauty, had provided a powerful grounding force that helped me reconnect with myself amidst the chaos of grief.

Your grounding practice will evolve as you do. Some days you'll need to stomp your feet and feel the earth beneath you, other days you might need to clear away energy that isn't yours. Trust your gut about what feels right in each moment. The goal isn't to escape your life; it's to be present in a way that feels safe and empowering.

As you continue practicing these skills, you're not just learning techniques, you're creating a whole new relationship with yourself and your world. That foundation of safety and presence you're building? It's going to support everything else on your healing journey.

Recap

Grounding is a powerful practice to reconnect with the present moment when trauma causes disconnection or overwhelming emotions. By using techniques such as creating a physical sanctuary, focusing on sensory awareness, and connecting with the breath, grounding helps reestablish balance and clarity.

This process also involves clearing your environment and protecting your energy, ensuring a safe space for healing. Through consistent grounding, you begin to create a foundation for emotional and physical stability in your journey.

In the Next Chapter

Next, we will explore the role of mindfulness. Learning how to live in the present moment is another critical skill for healing trauma.

5

Calm Waters

Mindfulness

Imagine standing on a beach, warm sand under your feet. Waves roll steadily, in and out. A breeze brushes your skin, carrying the smell of salt water from the ocean. The sun's heat shines across your shoulders, creating a comfort that is balanced by the ocean's cool embrace. It is a harmonious blend of sensations that gently lulls you into a state of restful awareness.

In this moment, something changes. The weight of your responsibilities, the noise of your busy thoughts, they all fade into the background. For just a moment, you're simply here, in the now. Not worrying about the past, not anticipating the future. The weight of your worries, the swirl of your thoughts, the tension in your body—all of it begins to quiet. You aren't trying to fix anything or get anywhere. You're just here, noticing each breath, each sound, each feeling as it comes and goes.

This is the essence of mindfulness. This is not an escape from your life, but a way to fully live in the present. It's learning to pause in the middle of a busy day and feel your feet on the ground. It's noticing the warmth of sun through a window, the taste of your morning coffee, the sound of rain on the roof. It's about learning to pause, be present, and truly experience each moment as it is.

Mindfulness invites you to engage in life without judgment, to notice what's happening right now, no matter where you are or what you're facing. Think of it as calm waters; steadily flowing and gentle, but still offering a peaceful refuge within your mind.

What is Mindfulness?

Mindfulness is the art of paying deliberate attention to the present moment with openness, curiosity, and without judgment. It's about being fully aware of your thoughts, emotions, sensations, and environment as they arise, without getting lost in distractions or reacting automatically.

Mindfulness encourages you to experience each moment exactly as it is—free from labels or expectations.

While many associate mindfulness with sitting in stillness or meditation, it is much broader than that. Mindfulness is an overarching practice that can be applied to any part of your day. It invites you to be present, whether you're eating, walking, talking, or even washing the dishes. It's about bringing attention to what you are doing, without rushing through it or being distracted by past or future concerns.

The Philosophy Behind Mindfulness

The philosophy of mindfulness is deeply rooted in Buddhist teachings, where it is known as *sati*. However, over the years, it has transcended its spiritual origins and has been adopted into mainstream practices for mental and emotional well-being. The essence of mindfulness lies in cultivating an awareness that doesn't judge or resist the present moment. Instead, it embraces whatever arises with acceptance and compassion.

In mindfulness, there is no goal of "doing it right" it's about experiencing life as it is, without the need to change or control anything.This aligns with a core principle in trauma recovery: embracing the present moment to regain a sense of control over what's happening within us, without trying to fix or escape it.

Mindfulness and the Brain
The effects of mindfulness on the brain are significant. Research has shown that consistent mindfulness practice can physically change the structure of the brain. For example, it has been shown to increase the size of the prefrontal cortex, the area of the brain associated with higher-order thinking, decision-making, and emotional regulation.

These changes enable you to process emotions more thoughtfully, make wiser decisions, and be more present in everyday interactions.

On the other hand, mindfulness has also been shown to reduce the size and activity of the amygdala, which is responsible for the brain's stress and fear responses. This reduction leads to decreased anxiety and greater emotional stability. For trauma survivors, this is especially beneficial, as mindfulness helps regulate the nervous system and counteracts the overactive fight-or-flight responses that often accompany trauma.

By shifting your attention to the present moment, mindfulness provides away to heal emotional wounds and manage stress in a calm, grounded way.

The Benefits of Mindfulness for Trauma Recovery
Mindfulness is particularly beneficial for trauma recovery because it provides a structured yet flexible approach to reconnect with your body and emotions without being overwhelmed by them. Here's how mindfulness can support trauma recovery:

- **Emotional Regulation**
  By cultivating awareness of your emotions without judgment, mindfulness helps you develop greater emotional resilience. You learn how to acknowledge and process your feelings instead of being controlled by them.

- **Reduction of Hyper-vigilance**
  Trauma survivors often live in a heightened state of alertness, constantly scanning for potential threats. Mindfulness helps calm this state by allowing you to be present and focused, reducing the need for constant

vigilance.

- **Reduction of Intrusive Thoughts**
  Mindfulness can help you notice when your thoughts are racing or becoming overwhelming, allowing you to gently return to the present moment. Over time, this practice can help reduce the intensity and frequency of intrusive thoughts.

- **Physical Healing**
  Mindfulness can help release tension stored in the body, allowing for relaxation and emotional relief. Many trauma survivors hold physical tension because of stress or traumatic experiences, and mindfulness encourages you to tune into and release these stored feelings.

Incorporating Mindfulness into Daily Life

Mindfulness doesn't have to be something you only practice in a formal setting. You can incorporate mindfulness into nearly every aspect of your daily life. Here are a few ways to make mindfulness a natural part of your routine:

Mindful Eating
Instead of rushing through meals or eating on autopilot, take time to really taste and savor your food. Pay attention to the textures, smells, and flavors. Notice the feeling of nourishment as you eat.

- **Mindful Walking**
  As you walk, slow down and pay attention to the sensation of your feet touching the ground. Notice the movement of your body with each step. Become aware of the sights, sounds, and smells around you as you walk.

- **Mindful Listening**
  In conversations, really listen to what the other person is saying. Instead of thinking about your response while they're speaking, focus entirely on their words, tone, and body language. This can improve your relationships and help you stay present.

- **Mindful Breathing**
  Whenever you feel overwhelmed, take a moment to pause and focus on your breath. This can be as simple as taking a few deep breaths, noticing the sensation of air filling your lungs, and gently exhaling. Incorporating mindfulness into daily activities helps you stay anchored in the present and promotes overall emotional well-being. You don't need to set aside hours for formal practice—small moments of mindfulness throughout your day can have a powerful impact.
- **Mindful Thought Observation**
  Take time each day to sit quietly and observe your thoughts without getting caught in them. Imagine your thoughts as clouds passing through the sky of your mind, you can see them, acknowledge them, but you don't need to chase or resist them. This practice helps develop a healthy distance from difficult thoughts and emotions.

Mindfulness Exercises for Different Situations

Mindfulness can be practiced in many forms, from brief exercises to longer, more immersive practices. Here are some examples of both short and longer mindfulness exercises:

Short Mindfulness Exercises

3-Minute Breathing Space

Sit comfortably and take a few deep breaths. For one minute, notice the physical sensations of your breath as it moves in and out of your body. For the second minute, focus on any thoughts or emotions that are present, simply noticing them without judgment. In the final minute, expand your awareness to the sensations in your body and the environment around you, grounding yourself in the present moment.

Mindful Observation

Choose an object in your environment and focus all of your attention on it for a minute or two. Observe every detail—the color, texture, shape, and even how it makes you feel. This can help you sharpen your awareness and stay present.

Longer Mindfulness Practices

Body Scan Meditation
Lie down in a comfortable position, close your eyes, and take a few deep breaths. Slowly bring your attention to different parts of your body, starting from your toes and moving upwards. Notice any sensations, whether pleasant or uncomfortable, and breathe into those areas to release any tension.

Mindful Walking
Go for a walk, focusing solely on your body's movements as you step. Pay attention to the rhythm of your breath, the movement of your legs, and the sensation of the earth beneath your feet. Try to stay present with each step, letting go of distractions.

Overcoming Common Challenges

It's common to encounter challenges when practicing mindfulness, especially when starting out. Here are a few tips for overcoming some of the most common obstacles:

Mind Wandering
Your mind will inevitably wander during mindfulness practice. Rather than getting frustrated, gently guide your attention back to your breath, body, or the present moment. This is a natural part of the process.

Restlessness
If you feel restless or impatient, acknowledge these feelings without judgment. Allow them to exist without trying to push them away. Over time, mindfulness helps you become more comfortable with discomfort.

Intrusive Thoughts
If disturbing or intrusive thoughts arise, simply notice them and return your attention to the present. Over time, you'll learn to create more space between yourself and these thoughts.

Recap

Mindfulness is a transformative practice that can support trauma recovery by helping you stay present, regulate emotions, and process difficult experiences. Whether through brief moments of awareness or more immersive practices, mindfulness can be integrated into your daily life to promote mental clarity, emotional resilience, and physical healing.

In the Next Chapter

In the next chapter, we will explore Meditation which is a structured form of mindfulness practice. We will dive deeper into different meditation techniques, their benefits for trauma recovery, and how you can incorporate meditation into your healing journey.

Gentle Flow

Meditation

Have you ever watched a river flow from the bank? Each bend and curve follows the path of least resistance, water flowing around obstacles rather than fighting against them. The river doesn't struggle or force its way; it simply moves forward, moment by moment, with unwavering presence and quiet determination.

Your mind can learn this same graceful dance.

In some of my darkest days, my thoughts would race and tumble like debris caught in rapids—accusations, confusion, and self-doubt colliding into one another until I felt I might drown in their chaos. Sleep evaded me. Peace seemed a distant shore I couldn't reach.

Then one morning, almost by accident, I discovered the simple power of sitting still. Not to empty my mind (an impossible task) but to watch my thoughts flow by without being swept away by them. Five minutes became ten. Occasional practice became daily. The river of my mind didn't stop (it never does) but I learned to sit on the banks rather than thrashing in its current.

Meditation isn't about achieving some mystical state of emptiness. It's about showing up for your life exactly as it is. It's noticing the weight of your body against the chair, the rhythm of your breath moving through your chest, the soft whisper of air against your skin. It's acknowledging thoughts as they appear without chasing after them or pushing them away.

This chapter offers simple, practical approaches to meditation that require no special equipment, no beliefs, and no hours of cross-legged discomfort.

These are practices for real people living messy, beautiful lives. People with jobs and families. People who sometimes forget to water their plants and occasionally eat ice cream for dinner.

The gentle flow of meditation meets you exactly where you are today. Not where you think you should be. Not where you hope to get someday. Right here, in this breath, in this body, in this moment.

Definition and Origin of Meditation

Meditation is a powerful tool for cultivating mindfulness and emotional well-being. It provides structured techniques that help still the mind, observe inner states, and ground yourself in the present.

Meditation has its roots in ancient spiritual practices, particularly within Buddhist traditions, and has revolved over centuries to become a widely recognized approach to managing stress, promoting mental clarity, and fostering emotional resilience. As with mindfulness, meditation invites you to engage in the present moment, but it often does so through a more structured and intentional practice.

Meditation can take various forms, from focusing on the breath to engaging in loving-kindness or guided visualization. What remains constant across these techniques is the goal of calming the mind, releasing tension, and nurturing a deeper connection to oneself.

Impact on the Brain
Meditation, much like mindfulness, has significant effects on

the brain. Through regular practice, meditation has been shown to enhance the prefrontal cortex, improving emotional regulation and higher-order thinking. This strengthened area of the brain allows you to process emotions more effectively, make thoughtful decisions, and engage with life more mindfully.

Meditation also helps reduce the activity of the amygdala, the brain region responsible for processing fear and stress responses. This reduction in amygdala reactivity allows you to experience less anxiety and greater emotional stability. For trauma survivors, these brain changes are particularly beneficial.

Meditation can help regulate the nervous system, reducing hyper-vigilance, intrusive thoughts, and emotional numbness. It creates a mental space for healing, allowing trauma survivors to observe their experiences without becoming overwhelmed.

Meditation for Trauma Recovery

Meditation offers a structured approach to trauma recovery, providing a mental space where you can process difficult emotions without becoming consumed by them. For trauma survivors, meditation can serve as a sanctuary—an emotional refuge that promotes inner peace and resilience. Techniques like loving-kindness meditation, body relaxation, and guided meditation specifically support trauma recovery.

These practices foster emotional healing by encouraging self-compassion, reducing stress, and promoting feelings of safety and connection. Through meditation, you can begin to heal emotional wounds, reduce trauma-related symptoms like hyper-vigilance and intrusive thoughts, and re-establish a sense of control over your mind and body.

For example, loving-kindness meditation invites you to direct positive and compassionate thoughts toward yourself and others, cultivating a sense of emotional connection and healing. Body relaxation techniques, such as progressive muscle relaxation, can help release stored tension in the body, promoting physical and emotional relief.

Guided meditations, particularly those involving safe place visualizations, allow you to mentally retreat to a place of calm, fostering a sense of security and safety during moments of emotional distress.

Practical Exercises
Meditation offers a wide range of exercises that can added to your daily routine. But first, creating a safe and comfortable environment for your meditation practice is crucial. Find a quiet space where you won't be disturbed. Consider reviewing Chapter 4 where we help you cleanse and set up this sacred space. Adding elements that promote relaxation, such as soft lighting, calming scents, or soothing music. The goal is to create a space that feels inviting and allows you to fully immerse yourself in the practice.

Loving-Kindness Meditation
Loving-kindness meditation is a powerful tool for trauma survivors. This practice involves silently repeating phrases of goodwill and compassion towards yourself and others. Sit in a comfortable position, close your eyes, and take a few deep breaths. Begin by directing kind thoughts towards yourself, repeating phrases like, "May I be safe, may I be happy, may I be healthy, may I live with ease." After a few minutes, extend these wishes to someone you love, then to a neutral person, and finally to someone with whom you have difficulties. This meditation fosters a sense of connection and compassion, helping to soften the edges of trauma and promote emotional healing.

Guided Meditation
Integrating guided meditations into your daily life can make a significant difference in your well-being. Guided meditation offers structured direction, making it easier to engage in the practice without worrying about what to do next. One of the most effective guided meditations for trauma recovery is the safe place visualization. This exercise invites you to imagine a place where you feel completely secure and at peace. Close your eyes and picture this safe place in vivid detail. It could be a real location, like a secluded beach or a cozy cabin, or an imaginary sanctuary.

Body Scan Meditation
Reconnecting with Your Physical Self

Body scan meditation is a practice designed to help you reconnect with your physical self, fostering both physical and emotional awareness. It involves paying close attention to different parts of your body, noticing any sensations without judgment. The purpose of body scan meditation is to create a deeper connection between your mind and body, promoting relaxation and self-awareness. For trauma survivors, this practice can be particularly beneficial. It allows you to tune into your body's signals, helping you identify areas of tension or discomfort that may beholding emotional pain.

- Lie down in a comfortable position, with your arms by your sides and your legs extended.
- Close your eyes and take a few deep breaths to relax.
- Slowly bring your attention to each part of your body, starting with your toes and moving up through your feet, legs, hips, torso, arms, neck, and head.
- Notice any sensations, such as warmth, tingling, tightness, or relaxation. If you feel tension, gently breathe into that area and allow the tension to release.

The practice of body scan meditation offers several specific benefits for trauma recovery. By reconnecting with your body, you can become more aware of how trauma has affected you physically.

Incorporating body scan meditation into your daily life can be a transformative practice. Set aside dedicated time each day for this exercise, even if it's just for a few minutes. Consistency is key to reaping the benefits of meditation.

Each time you engage in a body scan, you take a step toward understanding and alleviating the physical manifestations of trauma. This journey of reconnection and healing is about being present with your body, listening to its signals, and responding with kindness and care. Incorporate body scan meditation into your life and experience the profound benefits it can offer.

Calm Your Nervous System with Your Breath

Breath work is a transformative practice that taps into the body's natural ability to calm the nervous system. At its core, breath work involves consciously manipulating your breath to achieve a desired state of relaxation or alertness.

The science behind breath work lies in its profound connection to the parasympathetic nervous system, which is responsible for the body's "rest and digest" functions. When you engage in deep breathing, you stimulate the vagus nerve, which activates the parasympathetic response.

This process reduces the release of stress hormones like cortisol and adrenaline, helping to lower heart rate, blood pressure, and overall stress levels. As cortisol levels decrease, your body exits the state of chronic stress, allowing for healing and relaxation.

One of the simplest yet most effective breath work techniques is **diaphragmatic breathing**. Also known as belly breathing, this exercise focuses on breathing deeply into the diaphragm rather than shallowly into the chest.

This practice will calm your nervous system down in seconds.

Diaphragmatic breathing
This technique promotes relaxation and can be done anywhere, providing immediate stress relief.

- To practice diaphragmatic breathing, sit or lie down in a comfortable position.
- Place one hand on your chest and the other on your abdomen.
- Inhale deeply through your nose, allowing your abdomen to rise while keeping your chest relatively still.
- Exhale slowly through your mouth, feeling your abdomen fall.
- Repeat this process for several minutes, focusing on the rise and fall of your abdomen.

Box breathing is another powerful technique that can help calm the nervous system. This method involves breathing in a structured pattern, which can help regulate your breath and induce a sense of calm. To perform box breathing

- Sit comfortably and close your eyes
- Inhale deeply through your nose for a count of four
- Hold your breath for a count of four
- Exhale slowly through your mouth for a count of four
- Hold again for a count of four
- Repeat this cycle several times

The rhythmic nature of box breathing helps stabilize your heart rate and encourages a state of relaxation.

The **4-7-8 breathing technique** is another effective method for calming the nervous system and promoting relaxation. The extended exhalation helps activate the parasympathetic nervous system, encouraging a state of calm and relaxation. To practice 4-7-8 breathing:

- Sit or lie down in a comfortable position
- Close your eyes
- Inhale deeply through your nose for a count of four
- Hold for a count of seven
- Exhale slowly and completely through your mouth for a count of eight
- Repeat this cycle several times

Overcoming Common Challenges

Starting a meditation practice can come with challenges, particularly for those who are new to the practice or dealing with trauma. Common obstacles include difficulty staying focused, dealing with intrusive thoughts, and experiencing frustration or impatience.

Difficulty Staying Focused
Your mind may wander, and you might struggle to keep your attention on the breath or the present moment. This is normal, and it is part of the process. Meditation is not about achieving a state of perfect focus but about returning your attention to the present whenever it drifts. Each time you gently guide your focus back to your practice; you're strengthening your meditation "muscle."

Dealing With Intrusive Thoughts
For trauma survivors, intrusive thoughts can be distressing. When these thoughts arise, it's important to acknowledge them without judgment and then gently redirect your focus back to your breath or body. Over time, this practice can help reduce the intensity and frequency of intrusive thoughts, allowing you to regain a sense of control over your mind.

Impatience and Frustration
It's common to feel impatient or frustrated when starting a meditation practice, especially if you're not seeing immediate results. Each moment of practice, no matter how small, contributes to your overall healing and well-being. Be patient with yourself and allow your practice to unfold naturally.

By persevering through these challenges and incorporating meditation into your daily routine, you can create a space of calm, healing, and resilience. Meditation helps you stay grounded in the present moment, fosters emotional healing, and supports your journey toward mental clarity and peace.

Recap

Meditation is a powerful tool for calming the mind, regulating emotions, and reconnecting with the present moment. By focusing on breath, stillness, and intention, meditation helps to reduce stress and create inner peace. It allows you to cultivate awareness and presence, making it easier to navigate difficult emotions and memories. With regular practice, meditation enhances your ability to self-soothe and creates a deeper connection to your body and mind, supporting your healing journey.

In the Next Chapter

Next, we'll explore additional healing modalities like art therapy, sound healing and energy work to further support your recovery. These practices complement meditation and grounding techniques, offering new ways to release trauma and restore balance.

Visit our website where we have guided resources available tailored to different needs. Explore these options and find what works best for you. By making meditation a regular habit, you create a space of calm and self-awareness in your daily routine. This practice not only helps you reconnect with your physical self but also fosters emotional healing.

www.kandcompanyinc.com

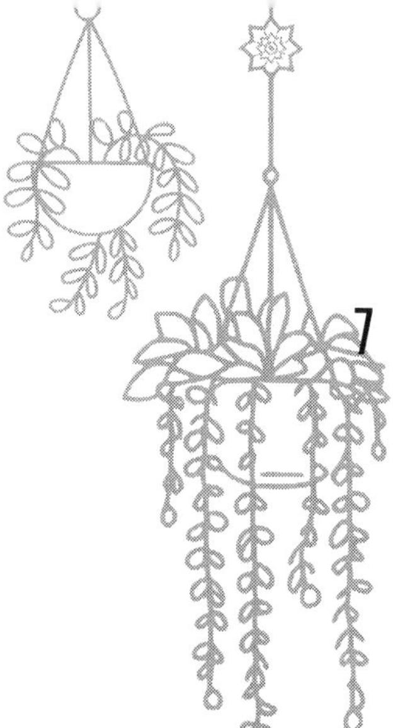

7

Nature's Medicine

More Healing Modalities

You walk into your bathroom at the end of a long, hard day. The soft, golden candlelight flickers, reflecting in the bubbles that froth you a warm bath. A gentle curl of steam rises, carrying the soothing scent of lavender and eucalyptus oils, each breath in feels like an invitation to relax.

You slide into the water; its warmth wrapping around you like a comforting hug, and your shoulders immediately ease away from your ears. In the background, a low instrumental melody drifts from a small speaker, mingling with the soft trickle of water.

Every sense is gently awakened: the dancing light, the calming fragrance, the silky touch of the water, and the tranquil rhythms that settle your thoughts.

In this chapter, we'll immerse ourselves in a variety of healing modalities like art, music, sound therapy, and aromatherapy, which will elevate the senses to create a sanctuary for emotional restoration.

Whether you're coloring your feelings onto a vibrant page, letting a sound bath resonate your body, or enjoying the lingering aroma of essential oils; each approach opens a passage toward understanding and release.

These sensory experiences are doorways to self-expression and emotional relief. Just as a warm bath soothes tired muscles, the creative and sensory tools you'll explore here offer powerful support for healing trauma.

Holistic Healing Exercises

In our journey toward healing and self-care, we often encounter physical, emotional and spiritual challenges that can feel overwhelming. However, there are various practices that can help us regain balance, restore our energy and promote a sense of well-being. These practical exercises include yoga, energy healing, aromatherapy, art therapy, sound healing, and journaling. They are all designed to support both our physical and emotional health.

Yoga

Yoga is an amazing tool for healing, offering a way to connect with your body, release tension, and foster mindfulness. The poses not only enhance flexibility and strength, but also provide a calming space for self-reflection and emotional release.

As you explore these yoga poses and healing techniques, remember that healing is a personal journey. What works for some may not work for others. Try to find the best practices that work for you.

Embrace each practice as an opportunity to connect with yourself and allow your body and mind to open up to the transformative power of these ancient practices.

Trauma-sensitive yoga practices are essential to create a safe and supportive space for those recovering from trauma. This means practicing in an environment where you feel secure and comfortable.

A trauma-informed yoga sequence can be transformative.

Start with breath work and a gentle warm-up to prepare your

body, followed by grounding poses like those listed below to establish stability and strength.

Let's explore some yoga poses that can help you find grounding, release tension and cultivate resilience.

Child's Pose
A calming and grounding posture that promotes a sense of security. To perform Child's Pose, begin by kneeling on the floor and sitting back onto your heels. Extend your arms in front of you and lower your torso toward the floor, bringing your forehead to rest gently on the mat. This position fosters a deep sense of support and safety, helping you release tension and connect to a feeling of inner peace. This is a great pose to start your day fresh out of bed.

Cat-Cow Pose
A beneficial sequence for releasing tension in the spine and enhancing flexibility. Start on all fours, with your wrists aligned under your shoulders and your knees under your hips. As you inhale, arch your back and lift your head and tailbone toward the ceiling (Cow Pose). As you exhale, round your spine and tuck your chin to your chest (Cat Pose). This flow helps release tension stored in the spine while promoting a fluid, relaxed motion throughout your body.

Legs-Up-the-Wall Pose
A deeply restorative position that enhances circulation and encourages relaxation. Find a wall and sit near it, then gently lie back and extend your legs up the wall. Rest your arms by your sides with your palms facing up. Close your eyes, take deep breaths, and allow the pull of gravity to ease tension from your legs and lower back. This posture helps you relax and can alleviate feelings of anxiety and fatigue.

Warrior II Pose
A powerful stance that fosters a sense of strength and resilience—qualities often diminished by trauma. Stand with your feet spread wide apart, turn your right foot out at a 90-degree angle, and bend your right knee over your right ankle. Extend your arms parallel to the floor and gaze over your right hand. Feel the strength in your legs and the openness in your chest, embodying a sense of courage and empowerment. Repeat the

pose on the other side.

Closing Your Yoga Practice
Finish with relaxation poses like Legs-Up-the-Wall Pose or Savasana, promoting deep relaxation and integration of the practice. By incorporating these yoga practices into your routine, you create a holistic healing experience that nurtures both your physical and emotional well-being. Yoga offers a pathway to reconnect with your body, release stored tension, and cultivate a sense of inner peace and resilience. It may feel better for you to start with an instructor, and that can be very beneficial. But starting on your own is also a great way to get moving.

Energy Healing

The Role of Reiki (ray•kee) and Healing Touch
Energy healing offers a unique approach to trauma recovery by focusing on the body's energy fields, specifically the chakras.

Reiki and Healing Touch are popular forms of energy healing aimed at restoring balance to the body's energy.

The body is surrounded by an energy field known as the aura, which can become disrupted by trauma and stress. When these energy fields are unbalanced, they can manifest as physical, emotional, or spiritual distress.

Chakras (which are energy centers along the spine described below) are essential to this healing process. Each chakra corresponds to different aspects of well-being, including security, communication, and love.

Root Chakra (Red)
Location: Base of the spine near the tailbone
Function: Stability, security, grounding, survival instincts.

Sacral Chakra (Orange)
Location: Just below the navel, in the lower abdomen
Function: Creativity, sexuality, pleasure, emotional expression.

Solar Plexus Chakra (Yellow)
Location: Upper abdomen, just above the navel and below the ribcage

Function: Personal power, self-esteem, confidence, willpower.

Heart Chakra (Green)
Location: Center of the chest, around the area of the heart
Function: Love, compassion, empathy, emotional balance.

Throat Chakra (Blue)
Location: Center of the throat, around the larynx and vocal cords
Function: Communication, self-expression, ability to speak one's truth.

Third Eye Chakra (Indigo)
Location: Middle of the forehead, slightly above the space between the eyebrows
Function: Intuition, insight, imagination, spiritual awareness

Crown Chakra (Violet)
Location: Very top of the head
Function: Spiritual connection, enlightenment, consciousness beyond the self

Balancing these chakras through energy healing promotes harmony and balance within the body.

In a typical Reiki session, you'll lie fully clothed while a practitioner gently places their hands either on or just above specific areas of your body. These placements correspond to chakras and other energy points.

The practitioner serves as a conduit for universal life force energy, allowing it to flow into your body. You might experience warmth, tingling, or even a gentle pulsation during the session. These sensations vary from person to person, and some may experience deep relaxation or even visual imagery.

The benefits of energy healing for trauma survivors are vast. It can provide immediate relaxation and reduce stress, calming the nervous system and promoting a sense of peace.

Over time, energy healing helps restore emotional balance, enabling you to process and release stored emotions. This practice also boosts the body's natural healing processes, enhancing immune function and supporting overall wellness.

Below are a few energy exercises you can try.

Self-Reiki Hand Placements

- Find a quiet and peaceful space.
- Sit or lie down comfortably and take several deep breaths to ground yourself.
- Gently place your hands over your heart, feeling the warmth and energy flowing through your palms.
- Hold this position for a few minutes, allowing the energy to flow into your heart center.
- Then, move your hands to your abdomen, repeating the process.
- Feel the nurturing energy spreading throughout your core.

This simple exercise helps balance your energy and promotes a sense of calm and well-being. You can practice this self-healing technique anytime you need to reconnect with yourself or when feeling overwhelmed. The beauty of Self-Reiki is that it's always available to you, requiring only your intention and a few moments of quiet attention.

Visualization of Healing Light

- Close your eyes and take a few deep breaths.
- Imagine a radiant light above your head, slowly descending through your body.
- Visualize this light as it fills each cell, bringing healing and comfort.
- As you breathe in, let this light flow through your body like warm honey, soothing any areas of tension or discomfort.
- With each breath out, imagine releasing anything that no longer serves you.

- As the light travels, envision it dissolving tension and negativity.
- Stay in this visualization for a few minutes, letting the healing light restore harmony and balance.

This practice can be especially comforting before bed or when you're feeling overwhelmed.

Chakra Clearing Visualization

- Sit comfortably, close your eyes, and focus on your breath.
- Begin by imagining a red light glowing brightly at the base of your spine where your Root Chakra is located.
- Feel this energetic ground becoming balanced and strong with each breath.
- Allow it to brighten and balance.
- Spend time here.
- Then, slowly move your focus up to your lower abdomen,
- Imagine an orange light in your lower abdomen where your Sacral Chakra is located.
- Allow this creative center to brighten and balance.
- Spend time here.

. . . continue through each chakra, visualizing the corresponding light of each color and their function, feel them becoming balanced and strong. Allow the light to grow stronger and more balanced, aligning your energy centers. As you move through each one, notice any sensations or insights that arise.

Root Chakra (Red) Tailbone, Grounding
Sacral Chakra (Orange) Lower Abdomen, Creativity
Solar Plexus Chakra (Yellow) Upper Abdomen, Power
Heart Chakra (Green) Heart, Love
Throat Chakra (Blue) Throat, Communication

Third Eye Chakra (Indigo) Forehead, Intuition
Crown Chakra (Violet) Top of Head, Enlightenment

Energy healing offers a gentle, effective way to address the effects of trauma. Incorporating these practices into your daily routine supports your body's natural healing process and fosters a deeper sense of inner peace and wellbeing.

Aromatherapy

Essential Oils for Emotional Balance

Aromatherapy harnesses the power of essential oils to promote emotional well-being. This practice works through the connection between the sense of smell and the brain's limbic system, which governs emotions and memories.

When you inhale the scent of essential oils, their molecules travel through your nose to the limbic system, triggering emotional responses that support healing. Essential oils can be used in various ways, including diffusion, where oils are dispersed into the air, and topical application, where diluted oils are applied to the skin.

Beneficial Essential Oils

Lavender is known for its calming effects, promoting relaxation and better sleep. You can diffuse lavender to create a peaceful environment or add a few drops to your bath for a soothing experience.

Frankincense, with its grounding properties, brings a deep sense of calm and spiritual connection. Diffusing frankincense during meditation enhances your practice and supports emotional balance.

Bergamot's up lifting citrus aroma is ideal for improving mood and reducing anxiety. Diffuse it in the morning or combine it with a carrier oil for a refreshing body lotion.

Roman chamomile is another powerful oil for calming the nervous system and promoting relaxation, especially before bedtime.

When using essential oils topically, remember to dilute them with a carrier oil to prevent skin irritation. The recommended ratio is about 6–12 drops of essential oil per ounce of carrier oil. Always check for potential side effects, especially if you are pregnant or have health concerns.

Aromatherapy Recipes

Relaxation Blend for Diffusion
Combine 3 drops of lavender, 2 drops of frankincense, and 2 drops of bergamot in a diffuser for a soothing and uplifting atmosphere.

Calming Bath Soak Recipe
Add 5 drops of chamomile and 3 drops of lavender to a tablespoon of carrier oil, then mix into a warm bath to help calm both body and mind.

Stress-Relief Roller Ball Blend
In a 10ml roller ball bottle, combine 2 drops of frankincense, 2 drops of bergamot, and 1 drop of chamomile. Fill with a carrier oil and apply to wrists, neck, or temples for instant calm.

Aromatherapy offers a natural way to nurture your emotional health, using the sensory experience of essential oils to support relaxation and emotional balance.

Art therapy

Creative Expression as a Healing Tool
Art Therapy provides a powerful outlet for processing emotions, especially when words fail to express what we're feeling. Through creative activities like drawing, painting, or sculpting, you externalize your emotions, which can help you understand and manage them.

This non-verbal method allows you to explore your inner world in a way that words sometimes cannot. Engaging in creative expression helps you discover hidden emotions and encourages self-exploration.

Whether through drawing, sculpting, or collage-making, each form of art provides a way to process complex feelings and deepen self-awareness.

Art Therapy Practices To Try

Visual Journaling
Create a visual journal where you can record your emotional state through drawings, paintings, or collages. This will allow you to track patterns and triggers in your emotional responses over time.

Mandala Drawing
This effective exercise promotes relaxation and meditation, helping you focus and supporting emotional healing. The circular patterns of mandalas can bring a sense of wholeness and completion.

Sculpting
This tactile approach provides a physical way to express feelings, bringing form to abstract emotions like anger or sadness. The act of molding and shaping materials can be both grounding and revealing.

Collage Work
Collecting and arranging images that resonate with you can help express complex feelings or experiences that are difficult to articulate in words alone.

Start with whatever medium feels most comfortable to you. Remember that art therapy is about the process rather than creating a polished final product. Allow yourself to express freely without judgment.

Music Therapy and Sound Therapy

Using Frequency for Emotional Release
Sound healing harnesses the therapeutic properties of frequencies to affect our emotional states. Music, sounds, and vibrations can influence our mood, reduce stress, and promote relaxation. Specific frequencies are known to have healing effects, especially when used to calm the mind or release emotional tension.

Sound Healing Practices

Music Therapy
Listening to calming music or nature sounds can create a serene atmosphere that helps lower anxiety. Creating playlists with pieces that resonate with you emotionally can be a powerful tool for self-regulation.

Vocal Toning
Singing or chanting, such as using mantras like "Om," can create calming vibrations that resonate deep within, helping to release emotional tension. The vibrations you create through your own voice can be particularly effective for self-healing. Visit our website for guided resources: kandcompanyinc.com.

Sound Baths
Participating in a sound bath, where you lie down and listen to gongs or tuning forks, allows the vibrations to penetrate your body, promoting relaxation and emotional healing. These experiences create waves of sound that wash over you, helping to clear energetic blockages.

Binaural Beats
Listening to specific frequency combinations through **headphones** can help synchronize brain waves, promoting deep relaxation, focus, or improved sleep depending on the frequencies used. By incorporating music and sound healing into your routine, you can use the power of sound to nurture your emotional well-being and restore balance. Even a few minutes of intentional listening each day can make a significant difference in your stress levels and emotional state.

Journaling

Begin by setting aside just 5-10 minutes each day for journaling. Choose a special notebook that feels inviting and keep it somewhere accessible. Don't worry about perfect writing or grammar—this space is for you alone.By incorporating journaling into your daily routine, you create a space for self-reflection, self-expression, and personal growth.

Therapeutic journaling provides a private space to explore your emotions without judgment. It helps you process complex feelings and identify patterns or triggers that may be affecting your emotional state. Through journaling, you can create a tangible record of your healing journey and gain clarity on your experiences.

Reflective Journaling
Take time to reflect on daily emotions and experiences, noting how they affect you physically and emotionally. Ask yourself what situations brought comfort or discomfort and why.

Stream-of-Consciousness Writing
Set a timer for 5-10 minutes and write continuously without stopping, allowing your thoughts to flow freely without editing or judgment.

Gratitude Journaling
Each day, write down three things you are grateful for, helping to shift focus toward positive aspects of life even during challenging times.

Letter Writing
Compose letters that you may never send—to yourself, to others, or to your past or future self—expressing thoughts and feelings you might not otherwise voice.

Artistic Journaling
Incorporate drawing, collage-making, or other visual elements to express emotions that might be difficult to capture in words alone.

Healing is a multi-faceted journey that requires addressing the mind, body, and soul as interconnected parts of a greater whole. True transformation happens when we acknowledge that healing is not a linear process but rather a dynamic unfolding—one that calls for patience, self-compassion, and an openness to exploring different modalities.

The grounding effects of yoga help stabilize the nervous system, reconnecting you with your breath and body in moments when past trauma may leave you feeling untethered. Reiki, a form of energy healing, works on a more subtle level, dissolving energetic blockages and promoting deep relaxation. Together, these practices create a strong foundation for healing.

Beyond movement and energy work, sensory-based therapies like aromatherapy, art therapy, and music healing further enrich your emotional and physical well-being. The scent of lavender or frankincense can calm the mind and ease anxiety, while creative expression through painting or journaling provides an outlet for emotions that words alone may struggle to convey. Music, with its vibrational frequencies, has the power to shift moods, regulate emotions, and even facilitate deep subconscious healing.

When you integrate these holistic practices, you cultivate a personalized healing approach, one that meets you where you are and evolves with you over time. Healing is not about finding one solution but rather weaving together different tools that support your journey in mind, body, and soul.

As you cultivate a deeper connection with yourself through holistic healing practices, the next step is learning how to extend that healing outward. Trauma often impacts our ability to trust others, form meaningful connections, and feel safe in relationships. Rebuilding trust, both in ourselves and in those around us, is a crucial part of the healing journey.

Recap

In this chapter, we explored a variety of healing modalities designed to support trauma recovery, such as art therapy, sound healing and energy work. These approaches help release stored trauma, restore balance, and promote healing at a deep, cellular level. Each modality offers unique benefits, whether through the vibrational frequencies of sound or energy work that clears blockages and recharges the system. Integrating these modalities into your healing journey allows for a more holistic approach to recovery, enhancing emotional, physical, and spiritual well-being.

In The Next Chapter

Stick with me as we explore the three-step approach to healing trauma. Things are getting good now!

Visit our website where we have many resources available. Explore different options and find what works best for you. By using various healing modalities regularly, you create a space of calm and self-awareness in your daily routine.

This practice not only helps you reconnect with your physical self but also fosters emotional healing.

www.kandcompanyinc.com

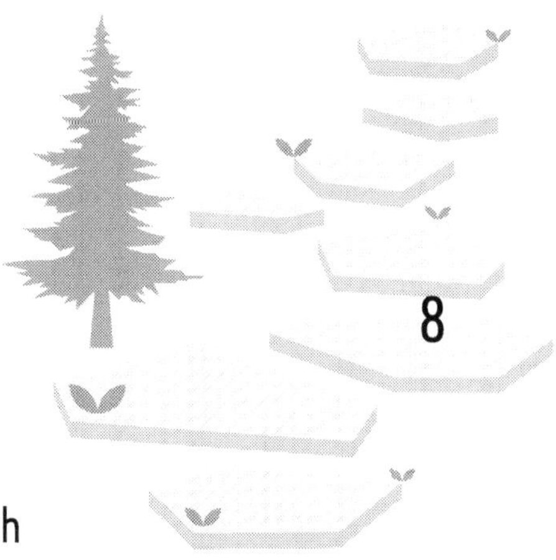

8

Blazing the Trail

The Three-Step Approach

The sunlight streamed through the gap in the curtains I should have opened hours ago. It's **11:42 AM.**

Outside my window, the mountains stood high against the cobalt blue sky, their peaks already dusted with early-season snow. Birds called to each other, their lively chorus at odds with the heaviness I felt.

I pulled the covers back over my head. Sleep had become both refuge and prison, where twenty hours could pass in an instant. My body's desperate attempt to avoid what my mind couldn't process. The memories still came in flashes; the helicopter ride to the hospital, my new born's hesitation at his first breath. The years that followed with a man whose cruelty only deepened after our son's birth; a husband who wore the mask of hero at his fire station but became a monster behind closed doors.

Through it all, I had known the presence of God. I had felt it in worship, witnessed it in my son's survival. My church community at Calvary had been my rock for years. Until everything collapsed at once.

The final escape from my abusive marriage.
My father's funeral.
Nowhere to call home.
A custody battle.

Four devastating blows in such rapid succession that I could barely catch my breath between them.

"*How could You allow this?*" I cried into my pillow, my prayer laced with betrayal.

But salvation didn't come from a place. Not from the church where I had once sought comfort, not even from the mountains outside my window. It came from something deep within me. Something that had always been there, waiting. My intuition. My soul, yearning for more answers, for a truth I could no longer ignore. To hear it, I had to strip away the noise.

The weight of others' expectations, the cycle of suffering I had unknowingly clung to; I had to create enough silence to hear my own voice. Only in that stillness, free from judgment and demands, did I finally allow myself to just be.

Me.

Not the version others wanted. Not the broken person I feared I had become. But the authentic soul that had been buried beneath layers of survival.

The mountains became my mirror, reflecting resilience back to me. How could something so vast and unshakable exist in a constant state of change? They further proved that beauty and harshness are not opposites but companions—like Yin and Yang. Healing isn't about escaping pain, but learning to move through it, just like a river overflowing with snowmelt. There's no space for yesterday's burdens, no time for past regrets, I found clarity. Life pulled me forward, demanding my full presence.

I began to sense the energy moving through all things. Connecting everything. This deeper awareness awakened my intuitive gifts. I realized that the same force flowing through mountain streams and snowy hillsides flows through us all, carrying the potential for transformative healing.

Energy work accomplished what prayer alone sometimes could not. It bypassed the thinking mind and spoke directly to the body's wisdom. Through it, I learned that healing isn't about erasing pain. It's about understanding it, integrating it, and allowing it to transform rather than define.

My journey through trauma and healing revealed a path that transformed not just my life, but the lives of countless others I've had the privilege to guide. Through energy work, a spiritual awakening, and a deep understanding of how our vibration shapes our reality, I discovered that healing follows a natural progression.

The Three-Step Approach to Healing Trauma

Finding Your Path to Wholeness

Healing from trauma doesn't need to be complicated. While the journey itself may have challenges, the path approach that provides clear guidance even when you feel overwhelmed or lost.

When I first began working with trauma survivors, I noticed how many tried to rush their healing or bypass their pain entirely. But true healing requires moving through the pain, not around it. The beauty of this approach lies in its simplicity. Each step builds on the one before it, creating a sustainable foundation for lasting transformation.

Think of these steps as a healing trail with three distinct landmarks: the Trailhead, the Trail, and the Summit.

STEP 1: Recognize & Regulate (Trailhead): Acknowledge your trauma and learn to calm your nervous system
STEP 2: Identify & Reframe (Trail): Discover and reshape the thoughts that emerged from your experiences
STEP 3: Transform & Reconnect (Summit): Use your insights to reshape meaning of your trauma and build connections

Let's explore each of these steps together.

TRAILHEAD: STEP 1
Recognize & Regulate

The first step in healing is significant: recognize the trauma you've experienced and learn to regulate your body's responses to it. This doesn't mean reliving painful experiences but rather acknowledging their reality and their impact on your life.

In my own journey, this meant acknowledging the terror I experienced during my car accident when we crashed at an estimated 120 mph. For decades afterward, I was terrified to ride as a passenger in any car. I minimized my reaction, telling myself I should "get over it now" or that my still present fear was "irrational". Recognizing my trauma meant finally admitting: "Yes, I experienced something genuinely life-threatening, and my body is still responding to that danger of that event."

Many of us have been conditioned to minimize our pain or compare it to others, thinking "it wasn't that bad" or "others have it worse". This denial only pushes trauma deeper, where it continues to affect us without our awareness. The truth is that trauma is personal. What impacts one person deeply might not affect another in the same way. Just know, your experience is valid, regardless of how it compares.

However, unrecognized trauma doesn't disappear. It manifests in unexpected emotional reactions, physical symptoms, relationship difficulties, and self-defeating behaviors. By bringing awareness to these habitual traits (patterns), you begin to loosen their grip.

Creating Safety in Your Body
Recognition must be paired with regulation. Before diving into the depths of trauma work, you need to know how to: Calm your nervous system when triggered Ground yourself when feeling overwhelmed Return to a window of tolerance where healing is possible (see Chapter 4) This is why coping skills from the earlier chapters are so essential. Without these skills, exploring trauma can lead to re-traumatization rather than healing.

In my case, I had to learn specific regulation techniques for car rides. Before getting into a vehicle as a passenger, I would practice deep breathing and remind myself of the present moment. During rides, I discovered that focusing on the passing scenery, instead of the driver's every move, helped ground me. When panic would ensue, which happened when the driver accelerated quickly, I would place my hand on my heart and silently repeat, "I am safe now. This is not the accident." followed by more deep breathing exercises. These simple regulation practices didn't eliminate my fear overnight, but they created enough safety for me to begin the deeper work of healing.

Step 1 Exercise
Recognition Journal

Begin a dedicated 'Blazing the Trail' journal with these exercises. *See my example from personal experience below the exercise.*

- **Choose one trauma to focus on initially.**
  What happened (briefly, without re-traumatizing yourself)
  How it has affected your life, relationships, and self-perception
  Physical sensations you experience when thinking about it

- **Pay attention to your body's signals during this process:**
  If you notice signs of overwhelm (racing heart, shallow breathing, numbness), stop and use a grounding technique
  Only proceed when you feel regulated and safe

- **Track your triggers for one week:**
  What situations, words, or environments remind you of the trauma?
  What physical sensations arise when triggered?
  Which regulation techniques help you return to balance?

Choose one trauma to focus on initially and write:

- **What happened (briefly, without re-traumatizing yourself):** *I was in a car accident many years ago where the gas pedal got stuck, and the car crashed into a ditch* *at high speed. I remember the feeling of helplessness as the car accelerated and the driver couldn't stop it.*

- **How it has affected your life, relationships, and self-perception:** *Since the accident, I've been extremely anxious as a passenger in cars. I've avoided long car trips and often make excuses not to go places if someone else is driving. This has limited time with friends who live far away. I've started to see myself as "too sensitive" or "high maintenance" because of these fears. My partner has been patient but sometimes gets frustrated when plans change due to my anxiety.*

- **Physical sensations you experience when thinking about it:** *When I think about the accident, my chest tightens, my breathing gets shallow, and my hands start to tingle. I notice my shoulders creeping up toward my ears and sometimes feel slightly dizzy, like I'm not fully in my body.*

- **Signs of overwhelm I experienced while writing**
While writing about the accident, I noticed my heart starting to race and my breathing becoming quick and shallow. I stopped writing and used the 5-4-3-2-1 grounding technique. After about 5 minutes, my breathing returned to normal, and I felt calm enough to continue.

- **How I made sure I was regulated and safe**
Before continuing, I placed my hand on my heart and took 10 deep breaths. I reminded myself "I am safe now" and felt my feet firmly on the floor. I also turned on some soft background music that helped me feel at peace.

Track your triggers for one week:
Monday
(trigger) Friend accelerated quickly after a stoplight.
Physical sensations: *Immediate tightness in chest, holding breath, gripping door handle until knuckles turned white. Regulation: Asked friend to drive more slowly, focused on counting passing trees, used deep breathing.*

Tuesday
(trigger) TV show with car chase scene.

Physical sensations: *Racing heart, sweaty palms, feeling trapped on the couch. Regulation: Muted the TV, got up and walked around the room, drank cold water slowly.*

Wednesday
(trigger) Conversation about someone else's road trip.
Physical sensations: *Stomach knotting, shoulders tensing, feeling disconnected from the conversation. Regulation: Excused myself briefly, ran cold water over my wrists in the bathroom, returned when I felt more grounded.*

Thursday
(trigger) Unexpected honking horn outside.
Physical sensations: *Startle response, racing heart, feeling frozen. Regulation: Named 5 objects I could see in my immediate environment, held a cold pack to my chest.*

Friday
(trigger) Had to take highway instead of back roads.
Physical sensations: *Shallow breathing, dizziness, tingling in hands. Regulation: Opened window slightly for fresh air, focused on slow breathing, listened to calming music.*

Saturday
(trigger) Dreamt about being in a speeding car.
Physical sensations: *Woke up sweating and heart racing. Regulation: Got up, moved to a different room and did some gentle stretching.*

Sunday
(trigger) I was the passenger in the car with a new driver.
Physical sensations: *Hyper-vigilance, muscle tension, feeling of dread. Regulation: Communicated my anxiety to the driver, focused on the horizon, alternated between deep breathing and engaging in distracting conversation.*

Patterns noticed: *Most triggers involve either actual car rides or unexpected loud noises. Physical sensations almost always start with chest tightening and changes in my breathing. Most effective regulation techniques are slow breathing, physical movement, and sensory focuses (especially cold sensations).*

Remember: Recognition without regulation can be overwhelming. When journaling, always pair awareness with soothing practices that help your body feel safe.

THE TRAIL: STEP 2
Identify & Reframe

Once you've created a foundation of safety through recognition and regulation, you can begin examining how trauma has shaped your thoughts and beliefs. Traumatic experiences often record powerful internal narratives that limit our potential and happiness.

Keep in mind that healing is not linear. You'll likely move back and forth between these landmarks as you move forward on the healing trail. There may be times when you need to focus primarily on regulation, and other times when you're ready to explore deeper meaning and connection.

After my car accident, I began to identify the thoughts that had taken root. Every time someone else drove, my mind raced with fear: "They don't know what they're doing," "We're gonna crash," and most terrifyingly,"We're gonna die. "The physical sensations were just as overwhelming as the thoughts. When a car would accelerate quickly or the driver needed to pass another vehicle, the g-force would instantly trigger my entire system. My heart would pound, my breathing would become shallow, and I'd grip the door handle until my knuckles turned white. These weren't just psychological reactions; my body was reliving the trauma.Overtime, I realized these thoughts and physical responses weren't random. They were direct consequences of the helplessness I experienced during those horrifying moments when the driver lost control. By tracking these reactions indifferent situations, I discovered how deeply this trauma had affected me. My fear extended far beyond cars; I had developed an intense aversion to any situation where I wasn't "in the driver's seat". For years afterward, even loud, unexpected noises would send me into a state of high alert.

These trauma-induced narratives took many forms in my mind:

- *"I can't trust anyone else to keep me safe"*
- *"I'm broken by this experience"*
- Always wondering when the other shoe is going to drop

These beliefs felt like absolute truths rather than perspectives shaped by painful experiences. The goal in this step is not to dismiss these thoughts, but to recognize them as protective adaptations that may no longer serve you.

The Power of Reframing
Reframing doesn't mean forcing positive thinking or denying real pain. Instead, it means gently questioning limiting beliefs and considering alternative perspectives that might be more accurate.

For example:

- *"I can't trust anyone" might be reframed as "Trust exists in layers; I can allow people different levels of trust based on their actions and our history together"*
- *"I'm broken by this experience" might become "I've been hurt but I am healing"*
- *I can transform the constant anticipation (the other shoe dropping) into mindful presence, focusing on what's happening right here and now, rather than what might happen.*

This process happens gradually through compassionate self-awareness rather than self-criticism or forced positivity.

With my car accident trauma, I slowly began to reframe my thoughts. "I have no control" became "I can choose who I ride with and communicate my needs." "We're going to crash" became "This is a different situation with a different driver and vehicle." The most powerful reframe came when I shifted from "I am helpless" to "I survived a crash, I am incredibly resilient and still here for a reason." These weren't just positive affirmations I repeated without believing; they were new perspectives I gradually came to recognize as equally true to my experience.

Step 2 Exercise
Thought Pattern Tracking

Create a table in your 'Blazing the Trail' journal with the columns below. See example below.

<u>Situation:</u> (What happened?) *Friend accelerated on the highway while I was a passenger*

<u>Automatic Thought:</u> (What went through your mind?) *"We're going to crash just like before. I'm gonna die."*

<u>Emotion:</u> (What did you feel?)
Terror, panic

<u>Physical Sensation:</u> (How did your body respond?) *Racing heart, shallow breathing, sweating, muscles tensed, nausea*

<u>Alternative Perspective:</u> (What else might be true?) *"The driver is paying attention. The car is functioning normally. The g-force I feel is a normal sensation of acceleration, not danger. I've ridden in cars thousands of times safely since my accident."*

<u>Supportive Response:</u> (How would you comfort a friend thinking this?) *"It makes perfect sense that I felt frightened after what I went through. My body was trying to protect myself based on my traumatizing experience. The physical reaction didn't mean I was in actual danger. I survived something terrible, and that shows incredible strength. I would take deep breaths, feel my feet on the floor of the car and repeat "I'm safe right now, and these feelings will pass."*

Create a fresh table and complete this for 1-2 weeks whenever you notice strong emotional reactions, particularly those that seem disproportionate to the situation (be sure to add in the final column and explanation as seen below). After this week, review your entries for patterns. Which core beliefs appear most frequently? How might these connect to your trauma history? Choose one recurring thought to work with each day.

Practice speaking the reframed version aloud while placing a hand on your heart, connecting the cognitive shift with physical comfort.

<u>Monday, 3:15 PM</u>
Situation: *Boss asked me to stay late to finish a project*

Automatic Thought: "*I have no control over my life. People always take advantage of me.*"

Emotion: *Anger, resentment, panic*

Physical Sensation: *Tight chest, clenched jaw, shallow breathing*

Alternative Perspective: "*I have choices even in this situation. I can negotiate the timeline or explain my boundaries.*"

Supportive Response: "*It's understandable to feel frustrated when my plans change. My time matters. What would help me feel more in control right now?*"

<u>Tuesday, 10:30 AM</u>
Situation: *Friend canceled lunch plans last minute*

Automatic Thought: "*I can't rely on anyone. I'll always end up disappointed.*"

Emotion: *Abandonment, sadness, irritation*

Physical Sensation: *Hollow feeling in stomach, heaviness in chest*

Alternative Perspective: "*Sometimes plans change for reasons that have nothing to do with me. This doesn't mean all people are unreliable.*"

Supportive Response: "*Disappointment is natural. This one cancellation doesn't define your entire friendship or all relationships.*"

Core beliefs are a fundamental, a deeply held conviction about yourself, others, or the world that you accept as absolute truth. These beliefs form early in life through experiences and messages we receive, and they operate like an internal GPS, guiding how we interpret situations and make decisions. It often happens without our conscious awareness.

Trauma powerfully disrupts and reshapes our core beliefs. When something traumatic happens, it can shatter previously positive beliefs or reinforce negative ones. For example, prior to my car accident, I was a confident young girl and after my car accident the core beliefs I developed were "I am never safe." or "Disaster can strike at any moment."

Core beliefs that appear frequently:

- *"I have no control in important situations"*
- *"I can't trust others to consider my needs"*
- *"I am helpless when others make decisions"*

Connection to Trauma History
These beliefs directly connect to the car accident where I experienced complete loss of control in a life-threatening situation. The helplessness I felt when the car accelerated uncontrollably has generalized to other situations where I perceive a lack of control.

SUMMIT: STEP 3
Transform & Reconnect

The final step involves transforming your relationship with trauma and reconnecting with yourself, others, and something greater. This is where healing becomes more than just managing symptoms. It becomes about growing through your experiences and finding renewed purpose.

Transformation happens when you begin to integrate your trauma into your life story, not as a defining feature, but as one chapter in a much larger narrative. This might involve asking questions like the ones I have mentioned are included below. I encourage you to ask yourself the same questions and journal your findings in 'Blazing the Trail' journal.

- How has this experience shaped who I am today?
  I've developed a heightened awareness of safety that in-

fluences how I approach various situations
I may value preparation and prevention more deeply than before
My relationship with uncertainty might have transformed
I may have greater appreciation for moments of safety and calm

- What strengths or insights have emerged from my healing journey?
  I've likely developed stronger emotional regulation skills from learning to manage panic and fear
  My resilience has been tested and strengthened through facing triggers repeatedly
  I may have gained deeper self-awareness about my thought patterns and physical responses
  My compassion for others' suffering may have deepened

- How might my experience help me connect with and support others?
  My first hand understanding of trauma responses makes me more empathetic to others struggling with similar challenges
  I can recognize signs of trauma in others that might be invisible to those without my experience
  The coping techniques I've learned might be valuable to share with others
  My story of healing can offer hope to those who feel permanently trapped by their trauma

These questions aren't about finding the silver lining to trauma, but about reclaiming your power to define what your experiences mean to you.

As I reflected on my car accident, I began to see how it had shaped my understanding of control and surrender. The experience ultimately led me to develop a deeper spiritual practice centered on accepting the inherent uncertainty of life. I also discovered that my heightened awareness of danger, while initially debilitating, eventually transformed into an intuitive ability to help others feel safe during difficult transitions. What began as atraumatic loss of control became, over time, a cornerstone of my approach to helping others navigate their own healing journeys.

The Healing Power of Connection
Trauma often leaves us feeling isolated and disconnected from ourselves, from others, and from any sense of meaning or purpose. Rebuilding these connections is essential for deep healing.

This reconnection might take many forms:

- Reconnecting with your body through gentle movement or visualization exercises
- Rebuilding trust in carefully chosen relationships
- Engaging with community in ways that feel meaningful
- Exploring spiritual practices that provide a sense of connection to something larger than yourself

Research consistently shows that social connection and a sense of meaning are among the strongest predictors of post-traumatic growth and resilience. When we feel connected, our nervous systems naturally move toward regulation and safety.

For me, reconnection happened in stages. First, I needed to reconnect with my body, which I had dissociated from during the accident. Yoga helped me slowly reclaim the physical sensations I had been avoiding. Then came reconnection with others. I joined an online support group where, for the first time, I didn't have to explain my fears. Most surprisingly, I eventually reconnected with driving itself. What had been a source of terror gradually transformed into a mindful practice, where I get to spend that time relaxing while enjoying the scenery by not being the driver.

Step 3 Exercise
Transformation and Connection

1. Spend time in nature regularly, even if just for 15 minutes. Notice and journal how your body feels in these natural spaces.
2. Write a reflection on how your trauma experience has influenced your values, strengths, or perspective on life.

3. Identify one way to connect with others authentically each week. This might be sharing something meaningful with a trusted friend, joining a support group, or taking a lunch break walk with people from work.

4. Explore practices that help you feel connected to something larger than yourself, whether through formal spiritual traditions, creative expression, or simply contemplating the night sky. This book is filled with endless possibilities.

5. Create a ritual to honor your healing journey. This might be lighting a candle or enjoying a back flow incense burner. This will mark your healing transition while engaging your senses.

One trauma healing ritual I found particularly meaningful with clients was to have them write a letter addressing the source of their trauma to the person, situation, or experience that addresses the source of the trauma. After expressing their unfiltered truth on paper, clients would choose between two symbolic release ceremonies: transforming their words through fire, watching their pain transmute into smoke and ash, or placing their letter into the earth or a flowerpot with flower seeds above it. These tangible experiences create powerful visuals of how something beautiful and resilient can emerge from their pain. After working these steps, the most significant obvious trauma in your life, practice each steps exercise on and daily basis finding patterns or deeply rooted experiences that you can "unpack" or rework through these steps.

Recap

These three steps create a sustainable path toward healing:

1. The Trailhead: Recognize & Regulate

2. The Trail: Identify & Reframe

3. The Summit: Transform & Reconnect

The landmarks attached to each step honor both the reality of the trauma and the possibility of growth beyond it.

Just like nature has its rhythm and flow, trust your own timing and needs. Some days, the most healing you will be able to manage is to reach out to a trusted friend. Other days, you might feel ready to challenge a long-held belief. Whatever phase you're in, approach yourself with the same compassion you would offer a friend.

The most powerful healing experiences happen when we combine honest awareness with true self-compassion.

In the Next Chapter

Next, we'll explore how fundamental self-care practices create the physical foundation that supports each step of this healing process.

Be proud of yourself for hiking this steep mountain. Like a determined backpacker you are tackling the climb one deliberate step at a time, facing steep terrain with courage, respecting your own pace, pausing when you need to catch your breath, and using your pack full of tools when the path gets rough. Don't forget to stop at the vistas to acknowledge how far you've come. Every step on the healing trail takes you to a higher perspective that will transform your life forever.

9

Clear the Air

Self-Care Best Practices

Outside my window the rain blurred into streaks of gray as the speedometer climbed. Sixty. Seventy. Eighty.

I was fifteen, riding shotgun down 26 Mile Road in Michigan. The first sign something was wrong came as a mechanical whine. The engine revving louder and louder even though my friend's foot had lifted from the gas pedal. "It's stuck," he yelled, his voice cutting through the roar as he slammed on the brake. But, nothing happened. The car sped forward instead of slowing, gaining with each passing second. Ninety. One hundred.

My fingers dug into the seat as my body instinctively braced. I knew the intersection well that we were approaching; cars crossing, unaware of the runaway missle we'd become. The thunder of the engine filled the car as the speedometer needle trembled past 110.

"Hold on," he shouted, turning the key to the off position. The engine died, but our momentum didn't. We were still flying, now without power steering, the wheel suddenly rigid beneath his hands as he fought to control our trajectory.

Then, everything went black. My next memory, the antiseptic smell of the emergency room, the strange disconnect of watching medical staff hover over a body I recognized as my own. I floated somewhere near the ceiling, oddly peaceful despite the chaos below. My pelvis had fractured in three places. Vertebrae compressed. Tailbone shattered. The doctors spoke in hushed tones to my parents: "likely paralyzed... may never walk again."

I didn't walk for nearly a year. Three weeks in the hospital blurred into months of bed rest, then a wheelchair, then crutches. I was an athlete before the accident, my body strong and resilient. I defied their prognosis, teaching myself to walk again after my bones were mended.

Life moved on. I moved on.

At least, I thought.

Eighteen years later, the pain began. Not as a twinge or a pulled muscle, but an agonizing dull ache that wrapped around my lower back and radiated through my pelvis and down the backs of my legs. It came without warning and stayed without mercy. The simplest movement of sitting down and putting on my socks became an exercise of endurance.

"We don't see anything mechanically wrong," the first doctor said, studying my MRI.
"You're lucky to be alive after a break like that. It's possible it's arthritis." suggested the second.
"Learn to live with it," advised the third.

Three different specialists. Countless tests. CT scans that mapped every millimeter of my spine, MRIs that hummed and clanked as I searched for answers, and X-rays that revealed nothing but properly healed bones.

Meanwhile, the pain intensified. I began to wonder if this was my life now. I was existing in a body that had become agonizing without relief. Dark thoughts crept in during sleepless nights. If this is living, what is the point?

Then I found him. A doctor who helped clear the air. He listened differently, he didn't dismiss what couldn't be seen. "Nerve damage," he said simply. "Scar tissue from the accident that damaged nerve endings, telling your brain you're in pain when everything is fine." The procedure was surprisingly straightforward too. Radio frequency ablation, essentially cauterizing the damaged nerve endings to stop their incessant false alarms.

When I woke up from the anesthesia, something felt different immediately. The constant ache and weight of the pain was gone, replaced by a surgical soreness that would fade with time. My body had been carrying the trauma of that accident for eighteen years, its resources slowly depleting like a storm I wasn't even aware was raging.

This is why self-care is vital. The basics we often take for granted: proper nutrition, restorative sleep, and mindful movement, aren't just about looking better or having more energy; they're about giving our bodies the resources they need to heal from trauma both seen and unseen.

When we understand trauma's physical dimension, we begin to see that caring for our bodies isn't separate from healing our mind and soul. It's the foundation upon which all other healing rests. The nervous system that gets dysregulated by trauma can't reset itself without proper nutrition. The brain that processes painful memories can't integrate without adequate sleep. The body holding tension patterns from past threats can't release without appropriate movement.

In this chapter, we'll explore diet, sleep, and exercise as essential trauma recovery tools. We'll learn how to listen to our bodies' wisdom and respond with what it truly needs, creating a condition where deeper healing naturally emerges.

Daily Self-Care for Trauma Recovery
Introduction to Self-Care

Healing from trauma requires a holistic approach that incorporates both mental and physical well-being. Daily self-care practices can help regulate emotions, reduce stress, and promote overall resilience. By focusing on key areas such as **nutrition, exercise, and sleep,** you can create a strong foundation for recovery.

Nutrition for Healing Trauma

Diets and Supplements for Emotional and Physical Recovery

The food you eat has an enormous impact on your emotional and physical recovery from trauma. Nutrients play a crucial role in brain health, influencing everything from mood to energy levels.

When you provide your body with the right nutrients, you support its natural healing processes. The brain, for instance, relies on a steady supply of vitamins, minerals, and healthy fats to function optimally. Specific nutrients like omega-3 fatty acids are essential for maintaining the structure and function of brain cells. Similarly, vitamins and minerals, such as B vitamins and magnesium, are critical for neurotransmitter production and neural communication.

A well-balanced diet can significantly influence your mood and energy levels. Foods rich in antioxidants, such as fruits and vegetables, help reduce inflammation, which is often elevated in individuals dealing with chronic stress or trauma. Inflammation can affect brain function, leading to symptoms like fatigue and depression.

By incorporating anti-inflammatory foods into your diet, you can help mitigate these effects and support overall brain health. Whole grains, lean proteins, and healthy fats provide sustained energy, helping to stabilize blood sugar levels and prevent the energy crashes that can exacerbate feelings of anxiety and irritability.

Several specific diets have been shown to be beneficial for trauma recovery.

The Mediterranean diet, rich in fruits, vegetables, whole grains, and healthy fats like olive oil, promotes overall health and well-being. This diet is known for its heart-healthy benefits, but it also supports brain health by providing essential nutrients that reduce inflammation and oxidative stress.

A plant-based diet can also be highly beneficial for trauma recovery. This approach emphasizes nutrient-dense foods like vegetables, fruits, legumes, and whole grains. These foods are packed with vitamins, minerals, and antioxidants that support brain health and emotional well-being. A plant-based diet can help stabilize mood and energy levels, providing a steady supply of nutrients that promote optimal brain function. Additionally, plant-based diets are often high in fiber, which supports gut health.

A healthy gut microbiome is linked to improved emotional well-being, as the gut-brain axis plays a significant role in regulating mood and stress responses.

Dietary Tips

1. **Incorporate More Whole Foods**
   Focus on eating fresh fruits, vegetables, whole grains, and lean proteins to support your body's natural healing processes. Shop the perimeter of the grocery store.

2. **Stay Hydrated**
   Drink plenty of water throughout the day to support cognitive function and overall well-being.

3. **Plan Your Meals**
   Prepare healthy meals in advance to avoid processed foods and maintain a balanced diet.

Exercise and Movement

Regular physical activity supports trauma recovery by releasing endorphins, improving mood, and reducing tension. Activities such as yoga, walking, or stretching can be gentle ways to reconnect with your body and relieve stress. Exercise not only strengthens the body but also has lasting effects on mental health, helping regulate stress hormones and improving resilience.

Find an activity that you enjoy and aim for consistent movement, whether it's a daily walk, a dance session, or structured workouts. When you engage in regular exercise, you not only boost your mood, but you also increase your energy levels, making it easier to cope with daily challenges. Movement can help you reconnect with your body, providing a sense of control and grounding that is often lost following traumatic experiences.

Gentle stretching and yoga are excellent starting points for trauma survivors. These practices focus on mindful movement and breath, helping to release tension and promote relaxation.

Walking or jogging in nature offers a dual benefit; physical exercise combined with the healing power of the natural world.

Dance and movement therapy provide a creative outlet for emotional expression. You don't need to be a trained dancer to benefit from this practice; simply put on your favorite music and allow your body to move freely.

Strength training and resistance exercises can also be beneficial for trauma recovery. These activities build physical strength, which can translate into a sense of empowerment and resilience.

Learning to listen to your body is important when engaging in physical activities. Recognize the signs of overexertion, such as excessive fatigue, dizziness, or shortness of breath. It's important to avoid pushing yourself too hard, especially if you're new to exercise or recovering from trauma.

Sleep Hygiene

Optimizing your sleep environment can make a significant difference in your sleep quality. Ensure that your bedroom is a sanctuary of comfort and tranquility. Invest in comfortable bedding that supports your body and feels inviting. Keep the room dark by using blackout curtains or an eye mask to block out light, which can interfere with your sleep cycles.

Maintaining a cool temperature in the bedroom can also enhance sleep, as a cooler environment is conducive to rest. Reducing noise levels with earplugs or a white noise machine can help create a peaceful atmosphere, minimizing disruptions that might wake you up.

Reading a calming book before bed can also help you unwind. Choose a book that is soothing and not too stimulating, allowing your mind to relax.

Limiting screen time and exposure to blue light is crucial. The blue light emitted by phones, tablets, and computers can interfere with your body's production of melatonin, a hormone that regulates sleep. Try to avoid screens at least an hour before bedtime, opting for more calming activities instead.

Enhanced cognitive function and memory are other significant benefits. Sleep plays a crucial role in memory consolidation and cognitive processing, making it easier for you to think clearly and make decisions. Quality sleep allows your body to repair and rejuvenate, boosting your immune system and overall vitality.

Prioritizing sleep is a powerful step in your trauma recovery, supporting your emotional and physical well-being. As you continue to explore the holistic approaches in this book, remember that sleep is a foundational element that can significantly impact your overall health and resilience.

Tips for Better Sleep

1. **Create a Relaxing Nighttime Routine**
   Wind down with calming activities like meditation, reading, or gentle stretching.

2. **Limit Screen Time Before Bed**
   Reduce exposure to blue light from phones and computers to support natural melatonin production.

3. **Maintain a Consistent Sleep Schedule**
   Going to bed and waking up at the same time each day helps regulate your body's internal clock.

By prioritizing sleep, you give your body and mind the best chance to heal and rejuvenate. Improving sleep hygiene begins with establishing a consistent sleep schedule. Going to bed and waking up at the same time every day helps regulate your body's internal clock, making it easier to fall asleep and wake up feeling refreshed. Consistency reinforces your body's natural rhythms, promoting better sleep quality over time.

Eco-Therapy or Nature Therapy

Eco-therapy, also known as nature therapy or green therapy, leverages the natural environment to support mental health and emotional well-being. This practice is grounded in the idea that spending time in nature can impact your mental state.

Nature has a powerful impact on mental well-being. Exposure to sunlight, fresh air, and natural surroundings can reduce stress and boost mood. Whether it's a short walk or time spent in a park, connecting with nature promotes healing.

Engaging in outdoor activities, such as hiking, gardening, or simply sitting in nature, can help regulate the nervous system and provide a sense of peace and balance. The connection between nature and mental health is well-documented, with natural settings offering a grounding effect that helps alleviate stress and anxiety. Just as a tree's roots stabilize in the earth, nature can provide a sense of stability and peace for you.

One of the most immersive forms of nature therapy is forest bathing, a practice originating in Japan known as **Shinrin-yoku**. This involves spending time in a forest environment, fully engaging your senses to absorb the sights, sounds, and smells of the woods. Forest bathing isn't about hiking or exercise; it's about being still and open to the natural world around you, allowing it to soothe your mind and body.

Gardening is another powerful eco-therapy practice. The act of nurturing plants and watching them grow can be incredibly healing. When you dig your hands into the soil, plant seeds, and tend to your garden, you're fostering growth and life. This process can mirror your emotional healing, providing a sense of accomplishment and connection to the earth. Gardening also offers the added benefit of physical activity, which can improve your overall fitness and well-being. Whether you have a small balcony garden or a larger outdoor space, gardening can be a therapeutic escape from daily stressors.

Nature walks offer a simple yet effective way to incorporate eco-therapy into your routine. Find a local park, trail, or nature reserve and take a mindful walk. As you walk, pay attention to your surroundings. Notice the colors of the flowers, the patterns of the leaves, and the sounds of the birds. This mindful engagement with nature helps ground you in the present moment, reducing anxiety and promoting a sense of peace. Walking in nature also provides gentle exercise, which can boost your mood and energy levels.

Outdoor meditation combines the benefits of mindfulness with the healing power of nature. Find a quiet spot in a natural setting, such as a park or garden. Sit comfortably and close your eyes. Focus on your breath, feeling the air enter and leave your body. As you meditate, listen to the sounds of nature around you, whether it's the chirping of birds or the rustling of leaves. This practice helps you connect with the natural world, enhancing your meditation experience and promoting a deeper sense of relaxation.

The serene environment of natural settings helps lower cortisol levels, reduce blood pressure, and promote relaxation.

Tips for Exercising Outdoors

- **Take a Daily Walk in Nature**
  Walking in a park or natural setting can reduce stress and improve mental clarity.

- **Try Outdoor Yoga or Stretching**
  Practicing yoga outside combines movement and mindfulness, enhancing relaxation.

- **Engage in Recreational Activities**
  Activities like hiking, biking, or gardening can provide both physical exercise and emotional balance.

To integrate nature into your daily life, consider creating a small garden space at home. Even if you don't have a large outdoor area, you can grow plants in pots or containers on a balcony or windowsill. Choose plants that bring you joy and require regular care, fostering a sense of connection and responsibility.

Schedule regular outdoor activities, such as weekly nature walks or forest bathing sessions, to ensure you spend time in nature consistently. Combining nature time with mindfulness practices, such as outdoor meditation or mindful walking, can enhance the benefits of both.

Recap
These practices offer a holistic approach to healing, connecting you with the natural world and promoting mental, emotional, and physical well-being. By focusing on a balanced diet, incorporating beneficial supplements, engaging in regular movement, prioritizing quality sleep, and connecting with nature, you can support your emotional and physical recovery from trauma. Self-care plays a vital role in healing, providing the foundation for overall well-being and resilience. Holistic healing modalities offer diverse ways to support your recovery.

In the Next Chapter

Next, we continue our journey through healing with more details on personal growth.

10

Rising Sun

Personal Growth and Resilience

As my hands trembled and my voice cracked, I struggled to find the words. The weight of my story felt too heavy. Each breath I took seemed like a battle against the fear that churned in my chest. In that moment, I was filled with uncertainty. The fluorescent lights seemed too bright, illuminating my vulnerability as I stood before a room of unfamiliar faces.

My heart raced and my mind spiraled with doubts: "Will they judge me? Will they see my vulnerability as a weakness?" But as I looked around the room, I didn't see eyes filled with judgment, I saw compassion and understanding. Some nodded gently, others leaned forward in their chairs, creating a silent space that somehow held my words with care.

In that moment, something inside me shifted. The weight of fear and shame began to lift. I realized that my vulnerability wasn't something to hide. It was something that others could relate to, something that invited connection.

I saw that sharing our pain doesn't make us weak; it makes us human, and it opens the door for others to do the same. It was the quiet "me too" whispered across tables and the gentle hand that reached for mine afterward that showed me how healing could flow in both directions when we're brave enough to be seen.

Soon after this experience, I enrolled in a MA program to become a clinical mental health therapist, driven by the realization that helping others find the same sense of validation and connection was my calling. I wanted to create safe spaces where others could experience the intense relief and strength I had discovered in vulnerability.

What began as a moment of terrifying exposure had become the first step on a path toward both healing and purpose. In facing my fears, I didn't just survive, I discovered a resilience I never knew I possessed that opened the door to a growth that would transform every aspect of my life.

Embracing Vulnerability
Steps to Open Up Safely
Vulnerability is often misunderstood as a sign of weakness, yet it holds profound strength. It is essential for emotional growth and healing, and it nurtures deeper, more authentic connections with others.

By being open and vulnerable, you invite others into your true self, fostering relationships built on trust, empathy, and understanding.

When we choose vulnerability, we allow others to see our unguarded selves, encouraging them to do the same. This exchange of honesty creates a supportive environment where both healing and growth can thrive.

Vulnerability also frees us to express our innermost thoughts and feelings without fear of judgment. In embracing this authenticity, we find strength. It allows us to acknowledge our struggles, our imperfections, and to build emotional resilience.

Journaling can become a safe space where you open up without the fear of judgment. The journey of embracing vulnerability begins with self-reflection and journaling. By setting aside time each day to write about your thoughts, feelings, and experiences, you begin to explore your emotional landscape. Reflect on moments when you felt vulnerable and how you responded. This practice can offer valuable insights into your emotional state and uncover patterns that influence your behavior.

Once you become more comfortable with self-reflection, consider sharing your thoughts with a trusted friend or confidant. Start by sharing small parts of your story with someone you trust who has shown empathy and understanding. Observe how they respond—this will help you gain confidence in opening up to others.

Boundaries create the safe space where you can express yourself without exposing yourself to emotional harm. Setting boundaries is another crucial aspect of maintaining emotional safety. Clearly communicate your limits and ensure they are respected by others.

As you embrace vulnerability, practicing self-compassion is key. Understand that this process takes time, and it's okay to take it step by step. Be gentle with yourself, acknowledging even the smallest progress along the way.

The fear of rejection and judgment often accompanies vulnerability. It's natural to worry that others might perceive you as weak or unworthy if they see your true self. However, authentic connections are born from honesty, not perfection.

Vulnerability requires courage, not weakness. It takes immense bravery to be open about your struggles and to accept your imperfections as part of who you are. Building confidence in vulnerability can be supported through positive self talk and affirmations.

Remind yourself that it's okay to be vulnerable and that your worth is not diminished by it. Repeating affirmations such as "I am worthy of love and acceptance" or "My vulnerability is a source of strength" can help reframe negative beliefs.

Embracing vulnerability is a transformative process of self-discovery and empowerment. It paves the way for deeper connections, allows for true self-expression, and fosters emotional resilience. By beginning with self-reflection, sharing your feelings with trusted individuals, establishing boundaries, and practicing self-compassion, you can harness the transformative power of vulnerability.

Vulnerability is not a weakness. It is a strength that unlocks the door to healing and growth.

Self-Discovery
Tools for Understanding Your True Self
Self-discovery is the journey of understanding your authentic self, and it is vital for personal growth and healing. The more you understand yourself, the more self-aware and authentic you become.

You begin to identify patterns in your behavior, recognize your strengths, and acknowledge areas for growth. This self-awareness empowers you to make decisions that align with your true values, leading to a more fulfilling life.

Authenticity means living in alignment with your true self, rather than conforming to societal expectations or the desires of others. By embracing authenticity, you uncover what truly matters to you—your personal values, passions, and motivations. This clarity helps guide you toward a life filled with purpose, satisfaction, and joy.

Reflective journaling is one powerful tool for self-discovery. Set aside quiet time each day to write about your thoughts, feelings, and experiences. Ask yourself reflective questions such as, "What do I value?" or "What activities make me feel most alive?" Journaling encourages deeper exploration and can help clarify your true desires and motivations.

Personality assessments, like the **Myers-Briggs Type Indicator (MBTI)** or the **Enneagram,** can also provide valuable insights into your personality traits, strengths, and growth areas. These tools help you understand how your mind works, how you relate to others, and how you can improve your interactions.

Life experiences, both positive and negative, significantly shape your identity. Reflecting on pivotal events helps you understand your emotional responses, strengths, and lessons learned. Overcoming a challenge, for example, might reveal resilience and determination, while positive experiences often highlight your passions and natural talents.

To deepen yourself-awareness, consider creating a life timeline. Chart key milestones, both good and bad, and reflect on how they've shaped your identity. This exercise gives you a holistic view of your life and helps you understand the deeper influences behind your actions and beliefs.

Building a vision board of your personal goals and dreams is another powerful tool for self-discovery. Collect images, quotes, and symbols that represent your aspirations, and display them where you can see them everyday. This visual reminder helps keep your goals in focus and motivates you to continue pursuing your true passions.

Exploring new hobbies or interests can also shed light on your passions. Pay attention to activities that make you feel excited or at peace. These experiences can offer deep insights into what truly resonates with your authentic self.

Building Resilience
Practices to Strengthen Your Inner Fortitude
Resilience encompasses mental, emotional, and physical strength. Mentally, it helps you maintain a positive outlook and stay focused on your goals. Emotionally, it allows you to handle stress and recover from setbacks. Rather than viewing setbacks as failures, view them as opportunities for growth. Learning from mistakes and staying open to new challenges helps build resilience over time.

Resilience is the ability to bounce back from adversity and grow from it. It involves transforming hardships into fuel for personal growth. True resilience isn't about avoiding challenges but facing them head-on with strength and grace.

Physically, it helps you stay strong in the face of challenges, ensuring your body can handle life's demands. Adversity is an essential component of building resilience. Each challenge you face teaches you valuable lessons about your strengths.

Nelson Mandela's resilience, after spending 27 years in prison, and Malala Yousafzai's courage after surviving an assassination attempt, are prime examples of how adversity can shape resilient leaders. Both used their hardships as a steppingstone to bring about change and grow stronger.

Resilience grows through practice. By adopting a positive mindset, building a strong support network, and maintaining physical health through self-care, you can fortify your resilience. Embrace challenges with an open mind and view them as opportunities for growth rather than obstacles.

To build resilience, start by reframing negative thoughts. When you encounter negative self-talk, challenge those thoughts. Ask, "Is this true?" or "What evidence do I have to support this?" Replace negative beliefs with positive affirmations like, "I am capable of overcoming this challenge" or "I have the strength to persevere."

The Power of Affirmations
Reprogramming Negative Beliefs
Affirmations are powerful tools that help you shift negative thought patterns. These positive statements influence your subconscious mind, reinforcing the belief that you are capable, worthy, and strong. By consistently practicing affirmations, you can create a self-fulfilling prophecy that shifts your mindset toward success.

The science behind affirmations supports their effectiveness. Studies show that self-affirmation activates the brain's reward systems, enhancing self-worth and reducing stress. Repetition is key to embedding these positive beliefs into your subconscious.

Create affirmations using present tense and positive language. For example, say "I am happy," rather than "I will be happy." Focus on specific, achievable goals, such as "I am thriving in my career and achieving my professional goals." Consistent practice is essential. Make affirmations part of your daily routine to reinforce these empowering beliefs. Over time, affirmations will transform your thoughts, actions, and ultimately, your life.

Celebrating Progress
Recognizing and Honoring Your Healing Milestones
Recognizing your progress is essential for motivation. Celebrating small victories keeps you moving forward and reinforces positive behavior. Milestones—whether big or small—are the building blocks of your growth. Consider using a progress journal to track your achievements.

Did you meditate for five minutes today? Celebrate it. Did

you handle a stressful situation better than before? Take note and acknowledge your growth. Set small, achievable goals and celebrate each success. This could involve treating yourself to something you enjoy or simply reflecting on your accomplishments.

A milestone chart or visual tracker can also provide motivation, allowing you to see how far you've come. Celebrating progress, no matter how small, helps maintain your motivation and reminds you of your capacity for growth. By tracking your achievements, setting goals, and reflecting on your journey, you honor your path and fuel your continued progress.

Vision Planning
Creating Your Future
Creating a personal vision starts with reflecting on your values and passions. Identify what truly matters to you and use that as the foundation for your vision. A vision board can serve as a visual reminder of your goals and aspirations, keeping them in focus.

Flexibility is essential in vision planning. Life can be unpredictable, and embracing change allows you to adapt your goals to shifting circumstances. Periodically revisiting and revising your vision ensures it remains aligned with your evolving values.

Create a detailed narrative of your future self. Describe where you see yourself in five or ten years—where you're living, what you're doing, and who you're with. This exercise clarifies your vision and makes it tangible. Develop an action plan with clear steps and timelines. Break down long-term goals into smaller tasks and hold yourself accountable by setting deadlines. Regular self-reflection ensures that you stay aligned with your goals, creating a vision for the future that drives clarity and purpose in your life.

In this chapter, we've explored the critical components of personal growth and empowerment: embracing vulnerability, engaging in self-discovery, building resilience, using affirmations, celebrating progress, and planning your vision for the future.

Each step in this journey strengthens your emotional fortitude and brings you closer to your true self. Personal growth is a continuous process. Stay open, embrace each moment, and celebrate the endless possibilities ahead.

Recap

Personal growth and resilience are key to overcoming trauma, as they involve building the inner strength to face challenges and grow from them. This process requires patience, self-awareness, and a commitment to healing. By embracing change and learning from difficulties, you develop resilience, which allows you to navigate life's ups and downs with more confidence and stability. As you grow, you become better equipped to handle future obstacles and cultivate a life filled with purpose and peace.

In the Next Chapter

In the next chapter, we will focus on rebuilding trust and creating emotional safety. Establishing a foundation of trust with yourself and others is vital for healing, and learning how to feel emotionally safe is essential for deepening relationships and fostering growth.

11

Growing Together

Rebuilding Trust and Creating Emotional Safety

The words blur at first, but as I read each line, their weight settles inside me. This entire mess—the lies, misunderstandings, accusations, and fractured relationships—all blamed on me. The betrayal cuts deeper with every paragraph.

"*How did it come to this?*" I whisper, burying my head in my hands.

The person I had trusted most, my support for the past few years had vanished without warning. No explanation. No final conversation. Just a gaping void where they used to be and in their place, an avalanche of chaos I never saw coming.

Trauma is a thief. It doesn't knock before entering. It doesn't ease you in gently. It crashes down like a tidal wave, pulling you under before you've even had a chance to come up for air.

I stood there, drenched in its aftermath, staring at the ruin left in its wake.

How had I missed the signs? How had I not sensed the shift in the tide? One moment, I was secure, held in the warmth of a relationship I believed was unbreakable. The next, I was gasping for air, struggling to comprehend how someone I had trusted with my life could turn on me so completely.

Betrayal is one of the deepest wounds trauma can leave behind. It shakes the very foundation of who we are, leaving us questioning not only the people around us but also our own judgement.

The sting of broken trust lingers, shaping the way we approach every relationship moving forward. We become hyper-vigilant, scanning for red flags, expecting the worst and preparing ourselves for another unexpected blow.

Even in the presence of love and care, doubt whispers in the back of our minds: *What if it happens again?*

Traumas most significant impact is often our disconnection from others. The experience creates invisible barriers leading to mistrust, emotional detachment and unpredictable reactions.

We find ourselves hesitant to reach out, uncertain how to navigate relationships that once came easily. We may even sabotage connections before they have the chance to hurt us.

Through my own journey, I have learned something powerful: while trauma may shatter our trust in others, it is connection that ultimately heals us.

Not only are healthy relationships possible after betrayal, they are necessary. They are the lifelines that pull us back to shallow water, reminding us of who we are beneath the wreckage.

I know this because, despite everything, one person in my life remained, my best friend. The one who saw me drowning and refused to let me go under. Her unwavering presence reminded me that not everyone leaves, not everyone betrays and not everyone stops caring when things get difficult.

Healing doesn't mean avoiding relationships, it means learning how to create ones that are safe, supportive and aligned with the version of ourselves that is emerging from the undertow of trauma.

In this chapter, we will explore the practical steps to to reconnect with both ourselves and others, fostering both the trust and emotional safety that trauma tries to drown. Reclaiming emotional safety and trust, both in ourselves and in others, create the foundation upon which we rebuild ourselves.

Trust can be rebuilt, love can exist without conditions, and here we show you how. While betrayal may have shaped our past, it does not have to dictate our future.

Impact of Trauma on Relationships

Trauma doesn't just change how we see the world; it changes how we see people. It alters our perception of safety, making even the most loving relationships feel uncertain. The people we once trusted without question can suddenly seem like potential threats. A simple disagreement might trigger a deep-seated fear of abandonment. A moment of emotional distance might be misinterpreted as rejection. We become trapped in a cycle of hyper-awareness, convinced that if we let our guard down, we'll be hurt again.

This is because trauma rewires the brain. You may recall in chapter one where we discussed the brain's response to trauma. The amygdala (the part of the brain responsible for detecting threats) remains on high alert, flooding us with stress hormones at the slightest sign of danger. Meanwhile, the prefrontal cortex, which helps us regulate emotions and think rationally, struggles to keep up. As a result, even minor conflicts can feel catastrophic, and trusting someone can seem impossible.

While trauma may shape how we respond to relationships, it does not have to define our future connections. We need to replace old survival responses with healthier, more intentional ways of relating to others.

Rebuilding Relationships

Before you can build healthy relationships with others, the relationship with yourself must be strong. Trauma can lead to self-criticism, feelings of unworthiness, and difficulty offering yourself the same compassion you extend to others.

The Impact of Trauma on Self-Trust

One of the scariest effects trauma can have is the erosion of trust in yourself. When your boundaries have been violated or your reality denied, you may lose confidence in your own perceptions, feelings, and judgment. This self-doubt can manifest in several ways such as:

- **Questioning your intuition**
  You might dismiss your gut feelings or second-guess your instincts; having learned that trusting yourself led to pain in the past.

- **Difficulty making decisions**
  Even small choices can feel overwhelming when you don't trust yourself to make the right call.

- **Seeking excessive validation**
  Without internal trust, you may constantly look to others to confirm your experiences or approve your choices.

- **Ignoring your needs**
  You might override your own needs or boundaries because you've been conditioned to doubt their legitimacy.

The path to rebuilding self-trust is neither quick nor linear, but it begins with recognizing that your relationship with yourself is the foundation upon which all other relationships stand. By learning to hear, honor, and advocate for yourself, you create the internal safety necessary for healing and growth.

Cultivating Self-Compassion

Self-compassion is the foundation upon which all healing rests. It involves treating yourself with the same kindness, concern, and support you'd offer a good friend.

When you make a mistake or face a difficult situation, self-compassion invites you to acknowledge your humanity and offer yourself understanding.

Try speaking to yourself as you would to a cherished friend

facing similar circumstances. Notice the difference in tone, in patience, in the willingness to see beyond momentary struggles to the inherent worth beneath. This shift in internal dialogue creates space for healing to begin.

Like a mountain stream that gradually smooths jagged rocks, self-compassion doesn't work overnight. It's a practice that becomes more natural with time and repetition. Each moment you choose kindness over criticism; you're reshaping the landscape of your relationship with yourself.

Healing from trauma isn't just about the experiences that happened to you; it's also about how you treat yourself in the present. It's about learning how to respect your emotional, physical, and mental space and, most importantly, how to protect yourself from further harm.

Rebuilding Your Emotionally Safe World

Emotional safety is like finding shelter in the mountains. A protected space where the harsh elements can't reach you, yet you still experience the beauty and vastness of the landscape around you. It's knowing that you can bring your authentic self, including your wounds, fears, and struggles, into a relationship without fear of judgment, rejection, or exploitation.

Creating emotional safety begins with careful observation. Who consistently responds to your vulnerability with empathy rather than criticism? Who makes space for your feelings without trying to fix, minimize, or outdo them? These are the people who can become allies in your healing journey.

In emotionally safe relationships, conflict isn't avoided, it's approached with respect and repair in mind. Disagreements are handled with care rather than contempt. Mistakes are addressed directly rather than through passive-aggressive behavior. Both people take responsibility for their impact on each other, regardless of their intentions.

For trauma survivors, emotional safety might include specific needs such as advance notice before touching, the freedom to leave overwhelming situations without explanation, or the ability to discuss triggers without shame. Communicating these needs clearly helps others create an environment where you can gradually expand your comfort zone.

Like finding your footing on a mountain trail, emotional safety allows you to venture further than you thought possible, knowing there's solid ground beneath you and someone who understands the terrain walking alongside you.

Building Emotional Safety:

- Validate emotions without rushing to problem-solve
- Respond to vulnerability with empathy rather than judgment
- Address conflicts directly without resorting to manipulation or contempt
- Honor each other's healing process, including triggers and coping mechanisms
- Practice non-judgmental curiosity about each other's experiences
- Make amends when you've caused harm, intentionally or not

Just as physical safety involves protection from bodily harm, emotional safety creates an environment where your authentic self can emerge without fear of attack, dismissal, or abandonment. This safety forms the bedrock upon which trust can gradually rebuild after trauma.

We need relationships that don't leave us walking on eggshells. A healthy connection means you don't have to fear explosive reactions or silent treatment when things get tough. It means disagreements can happen without the fear of being abandoned or punished. It means you can be yourself without constantly scanning for danger.

But emotional safety isn't about avoiding all discomfort or conflict, these are inevitable aspects of meaningful human connection. Rather, it involves confidence that even during difficult interactions, your essential worth and dignity will be respected.

Rebuilding Trust

Trust is the core of any healthy relationship, yet when trauma is involved, trust can feel like a steep mountain to climb. If you're anything like me, you probably have an ongoing battle between *wanting* to trust and *being terrified* to trust. When you've been hurt, especially by people who were supposed to protect you, trust feels like standing at the edge of a vast canyon, knowing you need to cross but seeing no bridge in sight.

Here's the truth: Trust isn't something you just decide to do. It grows slowly and it's perfectly okay if it takes time. For a long time, I thought trust had to be all or nothing. Either I trusted someone fully, or I didn't at all. But I've learned that trust forms in layers. You don't have to drop the rope on trust all at once. You can start small and let people prove themselves over time.

One of the most difficult lessons I learned about trust was to trust *actions, not words.* People can say all the right things, but if their actions don't match up, that's your answer. Pay attention to how people *show up* not just when it's easy, but when it's inconvenient.

Another hard but necessary lesson; not every discomfort in a relationship means danger. Sometimes, trauma makes us react to safe situations like they're unsafe because they remind us of something painful. Not every argument means the relationship is over. Not every mistake means betrayal.

Learning to pause and ask yourself, "*Is this my trauma speaking, or is this an actual red flag?*" can be clarifying and life changing. As you navigate your own journey toward trust, remember that patience with the process is essential.

Building the Capacity for Trust

The capacity to trust again doesn't emerge through determination alone but through a gradual accumulation of experiences that demonstrate reliability and safety.

Many trauma survivors oscillate between trusting too quickly (to avoid the vulnerability of careful assessment) and resisting trust entirely (to prevent potential betrayal). Building healthy trust involves finding middle ground, a discerning openness that allows connection while maintaining appropriate caution.

Components of Trust

Understanding trust as a multifaceted quality helps you rebuild it deliberately. Consider each layer to build upon but not in any specific order:

Reliability
Consistently doing what they say they'll do over time.

Honesty
Speaking truthfully, even when difficult.

Competence
Having the abilities needed for their role in your life.

Confidentiality
Respecting the privacy of what you share.

Emotional safety
Responding to vulnerability with care rather than exploitation.

Values alignment
Core beliefs and actions aligned with principles important to you.

Trust is not an all-or-nothing experience. It is built in small moments through shared experiences, honesty, and vulnerability. If you've been betrayed, it's natural to be wary, but opening up at a steady, manageable pace can help rebuild confidence in relationships.

Recognizing Safe vs. Unsafe Relationships

Not everyone deserves access to your heart, especially after trauma. Part of healing is learning to distinguish between relationships that nourish you and those that drain you. One of the biggest challenges after trauma is figuring out who is safe.

When you've been hurt before, your internal compass might feel off. You might second-guess your instincts, fear you're being too cautious, or wonder if you're overreacting. Things to be weary of:

Red Flags in an Unsafe Relationship
Hot and Cold Behavior - One day, they're all in; the next day, they pull away or disappear.
Dismissive or Manipulative Responses - They twist your words or make you feel like you're overreacting when you express your hurt or confusion.
Lack of Accountability - They never own up to mistakes and always shift the blame.
Control or Possessiveness - They make you feel guilty for having independence or friendships outside of them.
Feeling Drained - Instead of feeling safe and supported, you often feel exhausted or anxious after interactions.

A safe relationship won't make you feel like you're constantly questioning your own worth. Instead, it provides stability, allowing you to show up as your true self without fear of punishment or abandonment.

Remember that healing relationships after trauma is not a linear journey. There will be setbacks and moments of doubt. The important thing is to stay committed to your own wellbeing and to surround yourself with people who honor your healing process.

With time, patience, and intentional practice, you can create relationships that not only feel safe but also contribute to your continued healing and growth.

The mountain path may be steep, but with each step forward, you build strength and resilience that will serve you for the rest of your life.

Don't shy away from new people. Allow yourself to open up to new people. You could result in finding something true, real and consistent.

Journal Opportunities

As we close this chapter, consider these questions for deeper integration:

- In what relationship do you feel most emotionally safe and why?
- What does trust mean to you?
- How has past trauma shaped the way you trust people today?
- Do you tend to trust too easily, or do you struggle to let people in?
- Have you ever sabotaged a relationship because you were afraid of being hurt?

Let these reflections guide your focus as you continue developing the foundation for healing relationships in your life.

Recap

Trauma fundamentally changes how we perceive relationships, making safety feel elusive and trust seem dangerous. Healing begins with rebuilding trust in yourself through self-compassion, then extends to carefully creating connections where your authentic self can emerge without fear of judgment.

By understanding that trust forms in layers, distinguishing between trauma responses and genuine red flags, and recognizing the components of healthy relationships, you can gradually rebuild your capacity for meaningful connection.

Remember that this journey isn't linear, but with patience and intentional practice, you can create relationships that support rather than undermine your healing.

In the Next Chapter

As you continue your healing journey, the next chapter will explore how to build and maintain healthy boundaries and intimacy, both essential for fostering deeper relationships. By understanding and respecting your limits, you create the space for true connection and vulnerability to flourish.

12

the Birds and the Bees

Building Boundaries and Intimacy

Morning light spills over the ridge, casting a glow across the valley floor. The air hangs crisp, still, and cool. A narrow stream cuts through the banks, firm yet yielding, strong enough to contain the rushing current, yet open enough to allow movement and flow. Along the edges, wildflowers bloom, fragile, yet resilient, flourishing within the protection of their natural boundaries.In the distance, a storm gathers.

In the distance, dark clouds gather over one end of the valley. A storm approaches. You watch as rain lashes the mountainside and lightning splits the sky. Sometimes these storms carve new channels, uprooting trees and reshaping terrain. The valley does not resist; it absorbs, bends, reshapes. The mountains do not stop the storm, nor do they leave the land unguarded. Instead, they provide structure, holding space for change while ensuring the valley remains protected from complete devastation.

Nature demonstrates what trauma often forces us to forget, boundaries are not walls; they are the framework within which life thrives. Like the birds and the bees, we need both protection and connection. A beehive must be enclosed to function, yet open enough for pollination. A bird's nest must offer shelter yet still welcome the sky. Too much exposure, and life withers. Too much enclosure, and it never fully develops.

Healing follows this same wisdom. Trauma teaches us to build impenetrable barriers, to protect, to survive. But true intimacy requires a space both safe and permeable, where trust can take root. It is in this delicate balance between boundaries and openness that we rediscover what it means to be held, to be seen, to belong.

Perhaps healing isn't about avoiding life's storms or sealing ourselves off from potential hurt. Perhaps it's about learning to maintain our essential boundaries while still allowing nourishment in, trusting that even after an intense storm, something new always has the chance to bloom.

There is a beautiful paradox in trauma recovery. While trauma can profoundly disrupt our relationships, it's often through relationships that our deepest healing occurs. Those safe, supportive connections we form become the very soil in which trust can take root again. They create spaces where we can cautiously open our hearts and experience what it feels like to be truly seen, heard, and cared for.

Building Boundaries & Intimacy

Understanding Boundaries

Boundaries are essential for maintaining emotional, mental, and physical well-being. They are the invisible lines that define what is acceptable in our relationships and interactions. Trauma can blur our ability to establish these boundaries. When we've been hurt in the past, it can feel difficult to assert limits. We might have been taught to ignore our own needs or compromise for others, but learning to set boundaries is one of the most empowering acts we can take for ourselves.

Boundaries aren't walls, they're more like the lines that define a valley's edges, offering protection and direction while allowing us to breathe freely within the space. Without these boundaries, the landscape becomes unpredictable, and we risk losing our footing. The foundation of healing strengthens when we recognize and honor these edges within ourselves.

The first step in setting boundaries is recognizing where your limits lie. This requires quiet moments of reflection, listening to your inner sense of safety and discomfort. What situations or people leave you feeling drained or unsettled? Recognizing your needs may take time, but once the clarity comes, you'll understand where to draw your lines with confidence.

To start recognizing your needs, take time to reflect on your emotional state and your physical sensations. What do you need to feel calm, safe, and cared for? These needs are just as valid as anyone else's and acknowledging them is a step toward creating boundaries that honor your whole self.

After experiencing trauma, it can be hard to reconnect with your own needs. The survival mode that trauma instills often takes over, leaving us focused on just getting through the day. We may neglect our emotional, physical, and mental needs because we've been conditioned to do so to protect ourselves. Healing can strengthen when we stop ignoring our own well-being although, reconnecting with your needs may not feel easy at first, but with patience, you'll learn to better honor your needs. As time passes, you'll start noticing what brings you peace and what drains you, making it easier to set the boundaries you need.

Setting Healthy Boundaries

Once you recognize your needs, setting boundaries becomes an act of self-preservation. Boundaries are not about cutting people off or building walls; they are about defining where you feel safe, where you can give and receive without feeling drained. Start by setting small boundaries in relationships, and as you grow more comfortable, extend those limits to more challenging areas of your life. This might mean saying no to a social obligation that leaves you feeling overwhelmed or asking for space when you need it.

It's important to remember that boundaries aren't about controlling others they're about taking control of your own emotional well-being. By setting boundaries, you create the space necessary for healthy, balanced relationships. The more you practice and reinforce these boundaries, the more you will feel empowered and secure in your connections. If boundaries feel foreign or hard to set, start small rather than building a wall against those around you.

Here are a few practical ways to establish healthy boundaries:

- Practice saying "no" to small requests before tackling bigger boundary issues
- Use simple, direct language when setting a boundary: "I'm not comfortable with that"
- Notice when you're overextending yourself to please others
- Respect others' boundaries as diligently as you want yours respected
- Recognize that boundaries will evolve as your healing progresses
- Remember that healthy boundaries create the safety necessary for true intimacy

The Role of Boundaries in Trauma Recovery
Boundaries are particularly essential in trauma recovery. When we've experienced pain or mistreatment, our emotional systems become fragile, and without healthy boundaries, we risk being re-traumatized. Setting boundaries helps us reclaim control over our lives. By asserting ourselves and creating limits, we allow ourselves to heal in an environment that feels safe.

For example, imagine you're in a relationship where you often feel overwhelmed by the demands of the other person. Maybe they expect you to always be available, or perhaps they tend to dump their emotional stress on you without considering your needs. If you don't set boundaries, you could end up feeling exhausted, resentful, and emotionally drained.

On the other hand, by setting boundaries like, "I can't take on this emotional load right now, but I'm here for you in a different way," you protect your emotional health while still being supportive.

What Do Healthy Boundaries Look Like?
Healthy boundaries are clear, firm, and respectful. They don't have to be rigid or unyielding, but they do need to be com-

municated in a way that others understand. Setting boundaries doesn't mean cutting people off or being harsh.It's about taking care of yourself while respecting others. Healthy boundaries involve communicating your limits in a way that promotes mutual understanding and respect.

Healthy boundaries can manifest in several areas of your life:

- **Emotional Boundaries:** Knowing when to say no to emotional demands from others. This might mean distancing yourself from toxic relationships or limiting the amount of emotional labor you take on for others.

- **Physical Boundaries:** Protecting your body and space. This includes recognizing when you need personal space, when to say no to physical touch, or when to take time to rest and recharge.

- **Mental Boundaries:** Recognizing when you're being asked to engage in conversations or thoughts that don't serve your well-being. It's about recognizing when you need to step back from overwhelming mental demands or negative thinking patterns.

- **Time Boundaries:** Knowing how to manage your time and energy. This might mean saying no to commitments that don't serve you or limiting how much time you give to others, including work.·

- **Digital boundaries** establish guidelines around technology use, online communication, and social media engagement.

- **Self-Care and Boundaries**
  Self-care plays a vital role in maintaining healthy boundaries. Just as the valley needs time for the storm to pass before the land can settle again, you need to honor your own need for rest, rejuvenation, and reflection. Self-care helps you replenish your emotional and physical energy so you can continue to engage in relationships without feeling depleted. When you practice self-care, you are reinforcing your boundaries by showing yourself that your needs matter. Just as the valley flourishes when its edges are respected, your

well-being flourishes when you honor your own need for rest, nurturing, and self-compassion.

Intimacy and Trauma

Intimacy; the deep knowing and being known by another, is what gives relationships their meaning and power. It encompasses not just physical closeness, but emotional, intellectual, and sometimes spiritual.

After trauma, intimacy can feel frightening. Your nervous system might equate closeness with danger, causing you to withdraw when relationships start to deepen. It is important to know that this is a normal protective response, not a personal failing. Healing involves slowly expanding your capacity for intimacy at a pace that feels manageable.

Rebuilding intimacy after trauma takes time and patience. Emotional intimacy, which involves sharing your innermost feelings and thoughts, may seem overwhelming at first. But with trust and respect, intimacy can become a powerful force for healing. It's essential to create a space where both people feel emotionally safe to open up and share.

Keep in mind, building healthy relationships after trauma isn't about achieving perfection. It's about creating connections that support your healing rather than reopening wounds. With patience, practice, and self-compassion, you can develop relationships that not only withstand the impact of past trauma but help transform it into wisdom and strength.

Navigating Intimacy After Trauma

Intimacy is one of the most vulnerable aspects of human connection and after trauma, intimacy can feel especially difficult. The very act of being seen and fully accepted, of allowing someone into the depths of who we are, can feel like an impossible risk. Yet this same intimacy, when nurtured in safe and healthy relationships, becomes one of the most powerful healing forces.

Intimacy exists on a spectrum and encompasses several dimensions of closeness:

- **Emotional intimacy** involves sharing your inner experiences, feelings, dreams, and fears. This openness creates a sense of being known beyond surface presentations.

- **Intellectual intimacy** develops through sharing ideas, beliefs, worldviews, and values, creating connection through the meaningful exchange of thoughts.
- **Experiential intimacy** grows from shared activities and creates memories, building connection through common experiences that become part of a shared story.
- **Physical intimacy** includes not only sexual connection but all forms of wanted touch and physical closeness that create embodied connection.
- **Spiritual intimacy** emerges through shared exploration of meaning, purpose, and connection to something larger than oneself.

After trauma, certain dimensions of intimacy might feel more accessible than others. For example, you might find emotional vulnerability challenging but feel comfortable with intellectual exchange, or vice versa. This natural variation is part of the healing process. It's not a setback; it's simply your body and mind guiding you through the steps toward deepening connection. There's no rush. Take the time to explore and understand which type of intimacy feels safe to you in each relationship and gradually expand your comfort zone.

Healthy boundaries are essential to intimacy. Without clear limits, intimacy can become overwhelming and unsafe. Remember, just as a valley is shaped by its edges, intimacy is shaped by the boundaries that exist between two people. These boundaries allow the space for both partners to feel seen, heard, and understood without the fear of being overwhelmed or lost in each other. By understanding and respecting each other's boundaries, both people can create an environment where intimacy can unfold naturally. Like mist that slowly rises and reveals the valley's beauty, intimacy will also unfold gradually, its depth becoming clearer as the relationship matures.

You don't have to rush intimacy. In fact, taking your time to cultivate it with respect for your boundaries will allow the relationship to grow into something stronger and more fulfilling. Trust the process as it unfolds.

Healing and Rebuilding Intimacy

Rebuilding intimacy after trauma involves taking small, careful steps. Start by cultivating intimacy with yourself. Honor your own needs, acknowledge your boundaries, and practice self-compassion. Once you feel more grounded in who you are, you can begin to allow others into your life in ways that feel safe.

Intimacy doesn't happen overnight, but with time, you'll notice new depths in your relationships. Just like the mist rising gently over the valley, intimacy will gradually reveal itself, as the conditions you've cultivated create a space for connection to thrive.

As you move forward, remember that intimacy is built on trust, and trust is built through consistent actions, mutual respect, and an ongoing commitment to honoring your boundaries. Like the landscape slowly changing after a Spring rain, your intimacy will evolve, offering new insights and deeper connections as you continue your healing journey.

Moving Toward Thriving Relationships

As you continue to develop and heal relationships, remember that the goal extends beyond simply avoiding harm. True healing in relationships doesn't just mean surviving; it means thriving. Thriving relationships offer opportunities for mutual growth, joy, and a deepening of connection. It's about creating bonds that allow both people to expand, evolve, and flourish together.

Signs that you're moving toward thriving rather than (rather than just surviving) in relationships include:

- Feeling energized rather than depleted after interactions
- Looking forward to time together rather than feeling anxious or obligated
- Experiencing a growing range of emotions, including positive ones

- Finding yourself more present in interactions rather than emotionally distant
- Noticing increased capacity to navigate difficulties without crisis or disconnection
- Discovering new aspects of yourself emerge within the relationship's safety

Transformation doesn't happen overnight. Like the slow growth of a seed into a strong, vibrant plant, the shift from trauma-constricted relationships to life-giving connections unfolds gradually. Trust this natural process by continuing to cultivate the conditions where healing relationships can flourish.

Practical Exercises

Journal Prompt: Reflect on a time when you felt emotionally safe in a relationship. What boundaries were present that made you feel secure? How can you apply these lessons to other relationships?

Exercise: Think about one relationship where you want to improve intimacy. Start by identifying any boundaries that need to be reinforced, then communicate these boundaries clearly to the other person. How does it feel to set these limits and share your needs?

Recap
Now that we've explored the importance of setting healthy boundaries and fostering intimacy in relationships after trauma, it's clear that boundaries provide structure, safety, and direction, allowing intimacy to grow. By learning to recognize your needs, communicate your boundaries, and rebuild trust, you lay the foundation for deeper, more meaningful connections.

In the Next Chapter

In the final chapter, we will explore the exciting future of trauma research and the evolving approaches to healing. As new insights and methods emerge, the path to recovery continues to expand, offering hope and new possibilities for those seeking healing.

13

Beyond the Horizon

Future of Trauma Research

Envision stepping into a world where the mysteries of trauma are no longer hidden but where the brain's intricate response to pain and stress is mapped with precision.

Consider a future where healing is as tailored as a perfectly fitted tuxedo, with treatments designed specifically for your genetic makeup, neural patterns, and lived experiences.

Picture therapists working with tools that once seemed like science fiction: virtual reality sessions that guide you through past traumas safely, gentle magnetic pulses that awaken dormant neural pathways, or even therapies enhanced by ancient compounds like psilocybin (mushrooms), unlocking doors to suppressed emotions with care and precision.

This is no longer a distant dream. It's a reality taking shape before our very eyes. The field of trauma research is undergoing a revolution, driven by advancements in neuroscience, technology, and a deeper understanding of the human condition.

Scientists continue to discover how trauma reshapes the brain, while uncovering the secrets of resilience, and creating roads to recovery that were once unimaginable.

A Final Recap
The Impact of Trauma on the Brain

Recent research has shed new light on how trauma profoundly affects the brain, illuminating the ways in which traumatic experiences shape our neural landscape. When you experience trauma, it doesn't just leave an emotional scar; it creates tangible changes in the brain's structure and function. As discussed, studies have shown that trauma significantly impacts three key brain regions: the hippocampus, amygdala, and prefrontal cortex.

The **hippocampus**, responsible for forming and retrieving memories, often shrinks in size due to prolonged exposure to stress hormones like cortisol. This shrinkage impairs your ability to form new memories and can lead to fragmented or distorted recollections of the traumatic event.

Meanwhile, the **amygdala**, the brain's fear center, becomes hyperactive in response to trauma. This heightened activity results in an exaggerated fear response, making you more sensitive to potential threats. You may find yourself constantly on edge, easily startled, and struggling to feel safe even in non-threatening environments.

Lastly, the **prefrontal cortex**, which governs higher-order thinking, decision-making, and emotional regulation, also suffers. Trauma can reduce the activity and connectivity in this region, impairing your ability to manage emotions and think clearly while under stress.

Innovative Therapies and Future Directions

While traditional therapies offer invaluable tools for trauma recovery, emerging treatments and cutting-edge research are providing exciting new possibilities for healing.

Trauma doesn't just affect isolated brain regions; it disrupts the connectivity and communication between different neural networks. Functional MRI studies have revealed that trauma alters the brain's default mode network (DMN), which is active during rest and self-referential thinking. In trauma survivors, the DMN often shows increased connectivity with the amygdala, reinforcing negative self-perceptions and intrusive thoughts. This maladaptive connectivity makes it challenging to disengage from distressing memories and can perpetuate a cycle of rumination and anxiety.

The long-term consequences of trauma extend far beyond the immediate aftermath of the event. Impairments in memory and learning are common, making it difficult to retain new information or recall past experiences accurately. This can affect your daily functioning, from remembering appointments to learning new skills.

Moreover, trauma significantly increases the risk of developing mental health disorders such as anxiety, depression, and post-traumatic stress disorder (PTSD). The persistent state of hyperarousal and emotional dysregulation associated with trauma places a constant strain on your mental health, making it challenging to maintain a sense of balance and well-being.

Understanding these findings has significant implications for treatment. Early intervention is crucial for mitigating the long-term effects of trauma on the brain. Therapies that focus on reducing stress and promoting emotional regulation can help prevent further damage and support recovery.

Continuous support is equally important, as trauma recovery is not a linear process but one that requires ongoing care and attention. Tailoring therapeutic approaches to individual brain changes can enhance their effectiveness. For instance, mindfulness-based therapies can specifically target the prefrontal cortex, improving emotional regulation and reducing stress. Similarly, trauma-focused cognitive-behavioral therapy (CBT) can help rewire maladaptive neural pathways, fostering healthier thought patterns and behaviors.

The Role of Neurofeedback in Trauma Recovery

Neurofeedback is a fascinating and innovative approach to brain training that has shown promise in helping trauma survivors. At its core, neurofeedback involves monitoring brainwave activity and providing real-time feedback to help individuals regulate their brain function. This technique can promote improved emotional regulation, enhanced concentration, and better cognitive function, which are areas often impaired by trauma.

A typical neurofeedback session begins with the setup of sensors on the scalp, which monitor brainwave activity. This data is displayed on a computer screen, often through visual or auditory feedback. For instance, a calming video might play smoothly when the brain shows signs of relaxation, pausing if stress or distraction occurs. Over time, this process helps individuals adjust their mental state and rewire their brain for healthier patterns of activity.

Future Directions in Trauma Research

Advances in neuroimaging, such as functional MRI (fMRI) and diffusion tensor imaging (DTI), are offering unprecedented insights into how trauma reshapes the brain. These tools allow researchers to map the intricate networks that underlie thoughts, emotions, and behaviors, leading to more targeted and effective treatments.

Personalized approaches based on genetic and epigenetic factors also hold promise, tailoring therapies to an individual's unique biological makeup.

Practicing skills like compassion activates brain regions associated with empathy and emotional processing, particularly the **anterior cingulate cortex (ACC)** and the **insula**.

The ACC is involved in emotional regulation, decision-making, and empathy. When practicing compassion, this region becomes active, reflecting the mental effort to connect with others' emotions and experiences.

The insula is associated with interoception (awareness of bodily states) and emotional awareness. It plays a key role in understanding and sharing others' emotional states, making it critical for empathetic and compassionate behavior.

Neuroscientific studies, such as those involving **loving-kindness meditation** or **compassion training**, show increased activation in these areas when individuals engage in practices that enhance empathy and compassion. Over time, such practices can even lead to structural changes in these regions, promoting long-term emotional resilience and prosocial behavior.

By staying informed about these innovations, trauma survivors can remain empowered and hopeful. The future of trauma treatment is bright, with new discoveries paving the way for faster, more sustainable recovery outcomes.

As we continue to explore these frontiers, we move closer to a world where trauma no longer defines us but instead becomes a chapter in our story of resilience and growth.

Trauma has always been a formidable challenge, one that leaves deep imprints on the mind, body, and soul. For centuries, it was shrouded in mystery, misunderstood as a condition that shaped lives irreversibly. But today, as science and technology push the boundaries of what we know, the future of trauma research is filled with possibility. The innovations on the horizon are reframing our understanding of trauma while offering hope and power for healing.

Imagine a world where a scan of your brain can reveal the precise impact of trauma, mapping the disrupted connections and overactive fear centers like a detailed roadmap of your mind. This isn't science fiction—it's the promise of **functional MRI (fMRI)** and **diffusion tensor imaging (DTI)**.

These advanced imaging tools allow researchers to observe the brain's trauma response in unprecedented detail, uncovering how trauma alters communication between key areas like the hippocampus, amygdala, and prefrontal cortex. As these technologies evolve, they're making it possible to tailor treatments to each person's unique brain patterns, ushering in an era of personalized care.

Trauma doesn't affect everyone the same way, and researchers are delving deeper into why some people seem to recover while others struggle. The emerging fields of **genetics** and **epigenetics** are offering answers. Our genetic code plays a role in how we respond to stress, influencing traits like emotional resilience and sensitivity to trauma. But beyond genetics, epigenetics is revealing something even more extraordinary: the idea that our environment—our experiences, relationships, and even the stress we endure—can turn certain genes on or off, shaping how trauma manifests in our lives. This discovery is groundbreaking because it suggests that healing isn't just about overcoming what's happened but also about influencing the biological pathways that govern our response to it.

The promise of personalized trauma care doesn't stop there. Imagine a therapist examining your genetic and epigenetic profile alongside your brain scans, creating a treatment plan uniquely suited to your biology and history. This future isn't as far off as it seems. Clinical trials are already exploring the potential of combining this data with innovative therapies to transform the way we heal.

Emerging Treatments in Trauma Recovery

Cutting-edge therapies are also reshaping the landscape of trauma recovery:

- **Virtual Reality Therapy**: This immersive approach recreates traumatic experiences in a controlled environment, allowing individuals to process and desensitize themselves to triggers.

- **Psychedelic-Assisted Psychotherapy**: Substances like psilocybin and MDMA, used under strict therapeutic guidance, have shown promise in helping individuals access and process deeply buried trauma.

- **Brain Stimulation Techniques**: Non-invasive methods like transcranial magnetic stimulation (TMS) and transcranial direct current stimulation (tDCS) target specific brain regions to reduce symptoms of depression and anxiety while enhancing neuroplasticity.

One of the most exciting frontiers in trauma treatment lies in therapies that go beyond talking about trauma. The controlled use of **psychedelic substances**, like psilocybin and MDMA, is reshaping what we thought was possible in mental health care. In therapeutic settings, these substances help trauma survivors access suppressed emotions and memories, enabling breakthroughs that traditional therapies often take years to achieve. Early studies are showing remarkable results, with participants reporting significant reductions in PTSD symptoms after just a few sessions.

Similarly, **virtual reality (VR) therapy** is providing a novel way to process trauma. Picture a combat veteran entering a VR simulation that carefully recreates their traumatic experience in a controlled and supportive environment. With the guidance of a therapist, they can gradually desensitize themselves to the triggers that once dominated their lives, regaining a sense of control. This immersive approach is helping survivors rewrite their relationship with trauma, one carefully calibrated step at a time.

But perhaps one of the most remarkable advances in trauma treatment is the potential of **brain stimulation techniques**. Non-invasive tools like **transcranial magnetic stimulation (TMS)** use magnetic fields to stimulate areas of the brain affected by trauma, helping to regulate emotions and reduce symptoms of depression and anxiety. These techniques work directly on the brain's circuits, offering relief to those who have struggled to find it elsewhere.

Even as we explore these cutting-edge therapies, the focus is shifting to prevention. What if we could build emotional resilience before trauma strikes? Programs designed to teach stress management, emotional regulation, and social connection are being integrated into schools, workplaces, and communities. These initiatives aim to equip people with the tools to withstand life's challenges, reducing the long-term impact of traumatic events before they happen.

The integration of **artificial intelligence (AI)** is also transforming trauma care. AI algorithms are being developed to analyze patterns in large datasets, helping clinicians predict which treatments will be most effective for specific individuals. Apps and virtual mental health assistants powered by AI are offering support outside traditional therapy, making care more accessible to those who might otherwise go without.

Perhaps most inspiring is the collaborative spirit driving this field forward. Researchers, clinicians, and organizations around the world are working together to share knowledge and resources, ensuring that advancements reach the people who need them most. Trauma knows no borders, and the future of trauma research reflects a global commitment to healing.

On the horizon, the message is clear: the wounds of trauma no longer have to define us. With every discovery, every new therapy, and every step toward personalized care, we're moving closer to a future where recovery is not only possible but expected. The future of trauma research is a world where the power of healing trauma becomes the rule, not the exception.

The path forward is one of hope, where science, innovation, and compassion come together to help individuals reclaim their lives and write new chapters of their own resilience and growth.

Afterword

Healing from trauma is neither straightforward nor easy. Your path to recovery is unique, but the principles and exercises shared in these chapters offer a foundation for rebuilding your life.

Throughout this book, we have explored the complexities of trauma and its considerable effects on the mind, body, and soul. My intention was to help illustrate how these exercises can be incorporated into daily routines to foster inner peace and emotional regulation.

Holistic healing modalities such as specific Yoga poses, self-Reiki hand placement healing, various forms of art therapy and aromatherapy recipes provided diverse methods to address both physical and emotional aspects of trauma. Each approach offers unique benefits that can be tailored to your personal needs.

Getting started is all you need to do. These practices are not just therapeutic; they are transformative, offering a way to navigate life's ups and downs with resilience and grace.

Building healthy relationships and setting boundaries were essential topics. We have discussed the significance of trust, communication, and compassion. These elements are critical for creating a supportive environment where you can thrive emotionally and spiritually.

Embracing vulnerability, discovering your true self, building resilience, and using affirmations are all key components of anyones journey. Celebrating your progress and creating a vision for the future are vital steps in maintaining motivation and staying focused on your healing path.

Understanding the latest findings of the impact of trauma on the brain and exploring innovative therapeutic approaches like neurofeedback and virtual reality offer hope and astounding new tools for recovery, but there is nothing like a one-on-one session with a good therapist that you connect with or an intuitive energy healer. It's simply transforming.

Moving Forward

As you use the techniques shared in this book; remember that healing is continuous. It requires patience, self-compassion, and a commitment to your well-being, but healing is within you. Use the exercises shared and integrate them into your daily life. Start with small steps and gradually build upon them. Celebrate each victory no matter how small to acknowledge the progress you make along the way, because each step is that important.

I encourage you to take action in any way. Begin by setting 10 minutes aside each day then continue increasing as time allows. Start with practicing mindfulness and grounding. Get outside in nature, explore creative outlets, and connect with trusted individuals who can provide support along the way.

Seek professional help if needed and never hesitate to reach out for support. Your healing journey is not one you should walk alone.

Personal Note

In my own life, I have experienced trauma that had a significant impact. My experiences have re-shaped my life and led me to explore various healing modalities. I discovered that art therapy, mindfulness, being in nature, and spirituality have been the most instrumental in my healing and recovery. I hope the tools and techniques provided in this book offer you the same sense of peace and empowerment.

Sharing these insights has been a deeply personal endeavor. This book is filled with coping mechanisms that work, so keep it on hand for reference. Remember, you are not defined by your trauma. You have the strength and resilience to self-heal.

If you're looking for additional guidance and structure with healing from trauma, I invite you to look into the Power of Healing Trauma Workbook and Journal. I also plan to release online materials, such as the 21-Day Power of Healing Trauma Process Course. Both resources take the principles from this book and offer more guidance.

Embrace your journey with an open heart and mind. Be patient with yourself. You are worthy of love, happiness, and a fulfilling life. Keep moving forward, and trust in your ability to create a brighter future.

Thank you for allowing me to be part of your courageous transformation. May you find peace, strength, love and light,

Visit us *online for additional resources:*
www.kandcompanyinc.com.

Recommended Reading

Recommended Reading

This list provides additional resources for readers interested in deepening their understanding of trauma and healing approaches discussed throughout this book.

Understanding Trauma Science and the Brain

- Sapolsky, R. M. (2017). *Behave: The Biology of Humans at Our Best and Worst*. Penguin Press.
- Maté, G. (2011). *When the Body Says No: Exploring the Stress-Disease Connection*. Wiley.
- Cozolino, L. (2017). *The Neuroscience of Psychotherapy: Healing the Social Brain*. W. W. Norton & Company.

Neuroplasticity and Memory

- Doidge, N. (2007). *The Brain That Changes Itself: Stories of Personal Triumph from the Frontiers of Brain Science*. Viking.
- LeDoux, J. (2015). *Anxious: Using the Brain to Understand and Treat Fear and Anxiety*. Viking.
- Siegel, D. J. (2020). *The Developing Mind: How Relationships and the Brain Interact to Shape Who We Are*. Guilford Press.

Recognizing and Screening Trauma

- Herman, J. (2015). *Trauma and Recovery: The Aftermath of Violence--From Domestic Abuse to Political Terror.* Basic Books.
- Rothschild, B. (2000). *The Body Remembers: The Psychophysiology of Trauma and Trauma Treatment.* W. W. Norton & Company.
- Briere, J., & Scott, C. (2014). *Principles of Trauma Therapy: A Guide to Symptoms, Evaluation, and Treatment.* SAGE Publications.

Self-Care and Holistic Approaches

- Germer, C. K. (2009). *The Mindful Path to Self-Compassion: Freeing Yourself from Destructive Thoughts and Emotions.* Guilford Press.
- Dana, D. (2018). *The Polyvagal Theory in Therapy: Engaging the Rhythm of Regulation.* W. W. Norton & Company.
- Williams, M., & Penman, D. (2011). *Mindfulness: An Eight-Week Plan for Finding Peace in a Frantic World.* Rodale Books.

Mindfulness and Meditation

- Hanson, R. (2018). *Resilient: How to Grow an Unshakable Core of Calm, Strength, and Happiness.* Harmony.
- Kornfield, J. (2008). *The Wise Heart: A Guide to the Universal Teachings of Buddhist Psychology.* Bantam Books.
- Brach, T. (2012). *True Refuge: Finding Peace and Freedom in Your Own Awakened Heart.* Bantam Books.

Relationships, Boundaries, and Trust

- Perel, E. (2017). *The State of Affairs: Rethinking Infidelity*. Harper.
- Johnson, S. M. (2019). *Attachment Theory in Practice: Emotionally Focused Therapy (EFT) with Individuals, Couples, and Families*. Guilford Press.
- Brown, B. (2012). *Daring Greatly: How the Courage to Be Vulnerable Transforms the Way We Live, Love, Parent, and Lead*. Gotham Books.
- Aron, E. N. (2016). *The Highly Sensitive Person: How to Thrive When the World Overwhelms You*. Harmony.

Personal Growth and Resilience

- Southwick, S. M., & Charney, D. S. (2018). *Resilience: The Science of Mastering Life's Greatest Challenges*. Cambridge University Press.
- Joseph, S. (2013). *What Doesn't Kill Us: The New Psychology of Posttraumatic Growth*. Basic Books.
- Jampolsky, G. G. (2011). *Love Is Letting Go of Fear*. Celestial Arts.

Trauma Research and Future Directions

- Carhart-Harris, R. L., & Goodwin, G. M. (2017). *The Therapeutic Potential of Psychedelic Drugs: Past, Present, and Future*. Neuropsychopharmacology.
- Rothbaum, B. O., & Rizzo, A. (2019). *Virtual Reality for the Treatment of PTSD*. Annual Review of Medicine.
- Koek, R. J., et al. (2019). *Transcranial Magnetic Stimulation for Posttraumatic Stress Disorder and Major Depression*. Current Behavioral Neuroscience Reports.

This list represents a diverse range of perspectives on trauma healing, from neuroscience and somatic approaches to mindfulness and relational healing. Readers are encouraged to explore these resources as complements to the practices and insights shared within this book.

Made in the USA
Columbia, SC
12 May 2025